"In as controversial an area as eschatology, few are likely to agree with every last interpretation by the authors. But few books even try to say something on every teaching of Jesus about the future, in both the short and long term. *Jesus and the Future* does, and on the vast majority of texts it does so most persuasively. Written in a very straightforward and accessible style, this book is a must read by any who remain puzzled about this perennially intriguing topic."

—**Craig L. Blomberg**, Distinguished Professor of New Testament,
Denver Seminary

"Köstenberger, Stewart, and Makara have taken up a difficult and disputed subject—Jesus and the future—and shed light on many texts that are difficult and confusing for readers today. The book is marvelously clear and has a number of pertinent applications as well. The exposition of the Olivet discourse is particularly helpful."

—**Thomas R. Schreiner**, James Buchanan Harrison Professor of
New Testament Interpretation, Associate Dean,
The Southern Baptist Theological Seminary

"Unfortunately, apocalyptic prophecy, which is some of the most complex literature in the Bible, sometimes has gotten high-jacked by those who do not really understand what kind of literature it is, and what information it is trying to convey. In *Jesus and the Future*, we have a sane and sober look at the Olivet Discourse in Mark 13 and par. as well as other relevant material to get a grasp on what Jesus said about the near and more distant future, about the events of 70 AD and about the return of the Son of Man. In clear and lucid prose the authors carefully lay out the meaning of the relevant texts showing us that while Jesus provided us with more than enough information to give us 'an assurance of things hoped for and a conviction about things not seen' he did not provide timetables for prognosticators and calculators. God reveals enough of the future to give us hope, but not so much that we do not have to live by faith every day. This book deserves a wide readership."

—**Ben Witherington III**, Amos Professor of Doctoral Studies,
Asbury Theological Seminary; Emeritus Doctoral Faculty,
St. Andrews University, Scotland

"What did Jesus think about the future? Well, in this book the authors set out and lucidly explain what Jesus taught about the destruction of Jerusalem, the persecution of the church, his second coming in glory, the resurrection of the dead, and the final judgment. A cogent and easy-to-read account of what Jesus taught about the end times."

—**Michael F. Bird**, Lecturer in Theology at Ridley College, Melbourne, Australia

"Jesus and the Future is much-needed book on a topic that has been misrepresented and misunderstood like no other. Readers are treated to careful, competent interpretation of all the relevant passages of Scripture. The authors let Jesus and the biblical writers say what they want to say, not what many moderns want to hear. *Jesus and the Future* will go a long way in explaining an important doctrine at a level non-experts can access easily and yet experts will also find very helpful."

—**Craig A. Evans**, John Bisagno Distinguished Professor of Christian Origins, Houston Baptist University

"In this age when end-times issues are so popular and the debates are so divisive, a balanced and definitive work on Jesus' teaching on the issue is desperately needed. This work is very helpful and quite readable. I thoroughly enjoyed the coverage of the Olivet Discourse and was rather pleased at the comprehensive discussion of the other passages on the issue as well. It should be on the shelf of every Christian who wants to know about biblical eschatology."

—**Grant R. Osborne**, Professor Emeritus of New Testament, Trinity Evangelical Divinity School

"Jesus' Olivet Discourse is crucial to a biblical understanding of the end times, and it provides an authoritative framework for his teachings about the future scattered throughout the Gospels. This book examines and distills all this for us, patiently yet plainly guiding us through the biblical text—with care not to step beyond it. *Jesus and the Future* is marked by careful exegesis, theological awareness, simplicity, and clarity—this is eschatology as it ought to be done. It will doubtless prove to be required reading for any study of Jesus' great sermon on the end times."

—**Fred G. Zaspel**, Pastor, Reformed Baptist Church of Franconia, PA; Executive Editor, Books at a Glance; Adjunct Professor of Theology, The Southern Baptist Theological Seminary

JESUS *and* *the* FUTURE

JESUS and the FUTURE

Understanding What He Taught about the End Times

ANDREAS J. KÖSTENBERGER,
ALEXANDER E. STEWART &
APOLLO MAKARA

LEXHAM PRESS

Jesus and the Future: Understanding What He Taught about the End Times

© 2017 by Andreas J. Köstenberger, Alexander E. Stewart, and Apollo Makara

Lexham Press, 1313 Commercial St., Bellingham, WA 98225
LexhamPress.com

First edition by Weaver Book Company.

Print ISBN 9781683591641
Digital ISBN 9781683591658

Cover: Frank Gutbrod
Interior Design: Nicholas Richardson

We dedicate this book to our brothers and sisters in Christ
who are suffering for their faith all over the world:

"Therefore, humble yourselves under the mighty hand of God, that
He may exalt you at the proper time, casting all your anxiety on Him,
because He cares for you.

Be of sober spirit, be on the alert. Your adversary, the devil, prowls
around like a roaring lion, seeking someone to devour.

But resist him, firm in your faith, knowing that the same experiences of
suffering are being accomplished by your brethren who are in the world.

After you have suffered for a little while, the God of all grace, who
called you to His eternal glory in Christ, will Himself perfect, confirm,
strengthen and establish you.

To Him be dominion forever and ever. Amen."

(1 Peter 5:6–11 NASB)

Contents in Brief

Contents in Full

Preface

This book is written for readers just like you. It's not written for the experts and Bible scholars but for anyone interested in what the future holds, especially for Christians. *Jesus and the Future* is about what scholars call "eschatology," the study of last things. For many, when it comes to the end times, the Bible is a closed book, and sadly, scholars have contributed to this malaise. This is ironic because the Bible envisages an open heaven—not a closed book!—for Jesus' followers.

In this book, we'd like to do our small part to set people free from what you might call the "Babylonian captivity" when it comes to the Bible's teaching about the future. The original Babylonian captivity, of course, was Israel's exile in Babylon two and a half millennia ago. More recently, the term gained currency for the period preceding the Reformation when the papacy moved from Rome to Avignon in southern France as a sign of the church's growing corruption.

During both periods, God's people were in exile, whether literally or figuratively, in the sense that they were essentially shut out from what God had for them. Similarly, today many Christians are bewildered by the scholarly jargon and complicated end-time scenarios batted about by technical experts. Yet is reality truly as complicated? We don't think so. Once you've read this book, we hope you'll agree that knowing what the future holds for Christians is within our reach (though, of course, mysteries remain).

It is our hope that *Jesus and the Future* will equip you to cut through the maze of end-time teaching and to live your life in view of Jesus' teaching on the future. Jesus' teaching about the future is both simpler and more profound than many people realize. It is simple enough to be grasped by every Christian and it is profound enough to change your life. Living in the light of his coming is what the early Christians did. We believe that our prospect and expectation of the future can decisively shape our priorities, decisions, and conception of our mission. Let's see if with God's help we can bring greater clarity into this crucial area of our lives.

A book such as this does not come into being without the help of many individuals. The authors would like to express their gratitude to Jim Weaver for accepting this manuscript for publication and his expert shepherding of the project from beginning to end. We would also like thank our families and the institutions where we serve for their support and encouragement. This is truly a global project. We represent three different nationalities and serve on three different continents. What unites us is our faith in the Lord Jesus Christ and our firm expectation of his return. "Come, Lord Jesus!" (Rev. 22:20).

Abbreviations

AB	Anchor Bible
AnBib	Analecta Biblica
Ant.	*Jewish Antiquities*
BBR	*Bulletin of Biblical Research*
BCOT	Biblical Commentary on the Old Testament
BECNT	Baker Exegetical Commentary on the New Testament
B. Qam.	*Baba Qamma*
CBC	Cambridge Bible Commentary
CBQ	*Catholic Biblical Quarterly*
CCCS	Concordia Classic Commentary Series
ITC	International Theological Commentary
LCL	Loeb Classical Library
JSNTSS	Journal for the Study of the New Testament Supplement Series
NIBC	New International Bible Commentary
NICNT	New International Commentary on the New Testament
NICOT	New International Commentary on the Old Testament
NSBT	New Studies in Biblical Theology
OTL	Old Testament Library
PNTC	Pillar New Testament Commentary
SNTSMS	Society for New Testament Studies Monograph Series
TOTC	Tyndale Old Testament Commentary
WBC	Word Biblical Commentary
WTJ	*Westminster Theological Journal*
WUNT	Wissenschaftliche Untersuchungen zum Neuen Testament

Jesus and the Future

Jesus predicted the future. To some extent he would have been expected to do so since many of the common people of his day viewed him as a prophet in line with the prophets of the Old Testament.[1] In a moment of unintended comedy, a man named Cleopas unknowingly described Jesus to Jesus himself on the Sunday afternoon of the resurrection as "a man *who was a prophet* mighty in deed and word before God and all the people." He continued, "Our chief priests and rulers delivered him up to be condemned to death, and crucified him. But we had hoped that he was the one to redeem Israel."[2] Many viewed Jesus as a prophet, and some considered him to be *the* future prophet who Moses had promised would come.[3]

Biblical and modern history is littered with failed predictions of prophetic pretenders.[4] Time and events proved these prophets wrong. Some self-styled prophets keep their prophecies so vague that they cannot easily be falsified; nevertheless, over time they are usually exposed as imposters. But what about Jesus? Did he ever utter a prophecy that could be verified by history and either validate or falsify his claims? The Olivet Discourse contains just such a prophecy, a prophecy so bold and specific that his reputation would forever hinge on its fulfillment. Proper understanding of Jesus' words in this discourse is essential because many use it as the key to interpreting his other teachings about the future. In this book, we explore

---

1. Mark 8:27–28. Jesus describes himself as a prophet in Mark 6:4.
2. Luke 24:19–21. Unless otherwise noted, all biblical citations are from the ESV.
3. Deuteronomy 18:15, 17–19. See also John 6:14; 7:40, 52.
4. Examples could be multiplied; for example, see the infamous case of Edgar C. Whisenant, *88 Reasons Why the Rapture Will Be in 1988* (Nashville: World Bible Society, 1988).

all of Jesus' recorded teaching about the future, both regarding events that would take place later in the first century and events that are still future from our vantage point today.

Context

Before looking at the Olivet Discourse and Jesus' teaching about the end times in more detail, it will be important to understand the timing and significance of the discourse in his ministry. Jesus spoke the central prophecy contained in the Olivet Discourse on Tuesday afternoon during the final week of his life. It is also one of his longest recorded discourses and found in all three Synoptic Gospels: Matthew, Mark, and Luke.

It was the week before Passover, and Jerusalem was flooded with thousands of pilgrims from around the world who had come to celebrate the most important annual Jewish festival. The Passover was an annual commemoration of God's deliverance of the Jewish people from slavery in Egypt. It was a politically volatile time because the Jewish people longed for the day when God would raise up a leader to rescue them from Roman rule and oppression just as God had sent Moses to rescue them from Egypt. The Romans knew it was a perilous time and would bring in extra troops just in case some popular leader might try to whip the crowds into a riot or rebellion.

Jesus, knowing full well the implications and dangers associated with his mission, rode into Jerusalem on Sunday before Passover amidst a joyful crowd of Galilean pilgrims, introducing himself as Israel's long-awaited Messiah. The crowds, filled with messianic fervor, understood and responded by proclaiming him king.

Matthew 21:9*	Mark 11:9–10	Luke 19:37–38	John 12:13
And the crowds that went before him and that followed him were shouting,	And those who went before and those who followed were shouting,	The whole multitude of his disciples began to rejoice and praise God with a loud voice for all the mighty works that they had seen, saying,	So they took branches of palm trees and went out to meet him, crying out,

---

* Italics in biblical quotations are used throughout the book for the sake of emphasis and comparison.

Matthew 21:9	Mark 11:9–10	Luke 19:37–38	John 12:13
"Hosanna to the *Son of David!*	"Hosanna!		"Hosanna!
Blessed is he who comes in the name of the Lord! Hosanna in the highest!"	Blessed is he who comes in the name of the Lord! *Blessed is the coming kingdom of our father David!* Hosanna in the highest!"	"Blessed is *the King* who comes in the name of the Lord! Peace in heaven and glory in the highest!"	Blessed is he who comes in the name of the Lord, *even the King of Israel!"*

All four Gospels highlight the crowd's affirmation of Jesus' kingship. Earlier in his ministry, Jesus had carefully avoided overtly identifying himself as Messiah to discourage people from compelling him to be king. Now, however, he was openly accepting the title and role even though the Jewish religious leaders and the Romans would view this as a political threat.

On Monday, Jesus confirmed the Jewish leaders' suspicions when he cleared the temple of money changers and animal sellers.

On Tuesday, the same leaders confronted Jesus: "By what authority are you doing these things, and who gave you this authority?"[5] They rightly saw Jesus' actions as a challenge to their authority and were striking back. What made him think his authority was greater than theirs? Most of the day was taken up with challenges from groups who were trying to trap Jesus by his own words: questions about paying taxes to Caesar, the resurrection, and the greatest commandment.[6] These were not friendly debates; the opposition was actively trying to undermine Jesus' reputation and turn the crowd against him. Jesus' skillful answers further established his credibility in the eyes of his listeners. Jesus also went on the offensive by means of several parables (realistic stories with a veiled spiritual meaning) spoken directly against the religious leadership: the parables of the two sons, the

---

5. Matthew 21:23; cf. Mark 11:28; Luke 20:2; John 2:18.
6. Matthew 22:15–40.

wicked tenants, and the marriage feast.[7] These parables were not intended to teach nice moral lessons; they were conflict parables spoken to expose the religious leaders and identify them as the son who claimed to be doing the father's will while disobeying him, the wicked tenants who killed God's messengers and Son, and the man who would be barred from the messianic wedding feast.

Jesus climaxed his denunciation of the Jewish authorities who rejected him with a series of woes.[8] He already had plenty of enemies; his words here further increased their number, forcing confrontation. His whole ministry had been building to this point, and he actively engaged the Jewish religious leaders with his claims. At the end of the day, Jesus left the temple and prophesied its destruction. It is this prophecy that triggers the Olivet Discourse. It is also this prophecy that becomes an important bone of contention during Jesus' trial when witnesses claimed he had threatened to destroy the temple.[9]

Nothing much is recorded about Wednesday.

Thursday was spent in preparation for the Passover. That evening, Jesus celebrated Passover with his disciples, and by Friday evening he had been killed by an unholy alliance between the Jewish authorities and the Roman overlords—who variously distorted his messianic claims as blasphemous or politically subversive—and hastily buried in a borrowed tomb. Jesus' opponents appeared to have won; little did they realize how much they had lost.

First, the grave could not hold Jesus. He came back to life on Sunday morning, a week after his triumphant entry into Jerusalem as Israel's king. Thus, the crucifixion had proven utterly futile.

Second, Jesus' prophecy of the temple's destruction was fulfilled in the AD 70 when Roman armies razed Jerusalem and the temple in response to a Jewish rebellion. The Jews' effort to manipulate the Romans to their own advantage collapsed, and their nation and sanctuary were for all practical purposes wiped off the map.

This brief overview of Jesus' final week provides the context for understanding Jesus' words in the Olivet Discourse. The discourse was

---

7. Matthew 21:28–22:14
8. Matthew 23:1–36.
9. Matthew 26:61; Mark 14:58.

spoken on Tuesday after a long day of conflict and escalating verbal warfare. It is the longest discourse recorded in the Synoptic Gospels during Jesus' final week. Its length and central location make it the centerpiece of Jesus' instruction during this timeframe. All of this may seem straightforward—but what is difficult about the interpretation of this discourse?

Interpretive Views

As noted above, the Olivet Discourse begins with Jesus' prophecy that the temple will be destroyed. This pronouncement is tied to the fact that the religious leaders in charge of the temple had soundly rejected Jesus. The prophecy is the culmination of Jesus' response to their rejection and his denunciation of them. The disciples are shocked by Jesus' words and follow up by asking about the timing of fulfillment. When will the temple be destroyed?

Matthew 24:3	Mark 13:4	Luke 21:7
"Tell us, when will these things be, and what will be the sign of your coming and of the end of the age?"	"Tell us, when will these things be, and what will be the sign when all these things are about to be accomplished?"	"Teacher, when will these things be, and what will be the sign when these things are about to take place?"

The question is expanded in Matthew to include Jesus' "coming [Greek *parousia*] and . . . the end of the age." Jesus answers their question with the Olivet Discourse. Near the end of the discourse in each Gospel, Jesus utters these solemn words:

Matthew 24:34	Mark 13:30	Luke 21:32
Truly, I say to you, *this generation* will not pass away until all these things take place.	Truly, I say to you, *this generation* will not pass away until all these things take place.	Truly, I say to you, *this generation* will not pass away until all has taken place.

This is still quite straightforward; the temple would be destroyed in judgment during the lifetime of that generation. This is indeed what happened in the year 70. Things get complicated, however, when we begin to look at the details. Shortly before the statement about "this generation," Jesus seems to indicate that the temple's destruction will be followed immediately by cosmic upheaval and his return.

Matthew 24:29–31	Mark 13:24–27	Luke 21:25–28
"Immediately after the tribulation of those days the sun will be darkened, and the moon will not give its light, and the stars will fall from heaven,	*"But in those days, after that tribulation*, the sun will be darkened, and the moon will not give its light, [25] and the stars will be falling from heaven,	"And there will be signs in sun and moon and stars, and on the earth distress of nations in perplexity because of the roaring of the sea and the waves, [26] people fainting with fear and with foreboding of what is coming on the world. For the powers of the
and the powers of the heavens will be shaken.	and the powers in the heavens will be shaken.	heavens will be shaken.
[30] *. . . and they will see the Son of Man coming on the clouds of heaven with power and great glory.*	[26] *And then they will see the Son of Man coming in clouds with great power and glory.*	[27] *And then they will see the Son of Man coming in a cloud with power and great glory.*
[31] And he will send out his angels with a loud trumpet call, and they will gather his elect from the four winds, from one end of heaven to the other.	[27] And then he will send out the angels and gather his elect from the four winds, from the ends of the earth to the ends of heaven.	[28] Now when these things begin to take place, straighten up and raise your heads, because your redemption is drawing near."

This leads to the main interpretive difficulty associated with the Olivet Discourse: Jesus seems to indicate that the temple will be destroyed and he will return within that generation. Interpreters have responded in several ways. First, some claim that this is indeed what Jesus predicted and he was simply wrong, like all the other prophets who issued predictions regarding the world coming to an end. Most Christians—including the present authors—don't find this solution satisfactory for many reasons, foremost the public vindication of Jesus by God through resurrection.[10] The resurrection forms the basis for the Christian beliefs about Jesus expressed throughout the New Testament, beliefs that do not include the possibility of Jesus being a failed prophet.[11]

Second, some interpreters try to reinterpret Jesus' statement about "this generation" to provide room for the return of Christ long after the period of that generation. This approach takes the language of Jesus' return literally and is expressed, for example, in the popular Left Behind book series by Tim LaHaye and Jerry Jenkins. In this view, Jesus doesn't really answer the disciples' initial question about the timing of the destruction of the temple—he basically ignores it to talk about events that will occur thousands of years later.

Third, other (preterist) interpreters try to reinterpret Jesus' apparent prophecy of cosmic upheaval and his return so that everything spoken by Jesus in the Olivet Discourse can be said to be fulfilled in the Roman destruction of Jerusalem and the temple in the year 70.

Fourth, many others are confused or uncertain as to what Jesus meant. They recognize that he seems to be speaking of two distinct events in time: the destruction of the temple and his future return. But when is he talking about one and when about the other, and how can you tell? It is at this point that the Olivet Discourse becomes puzzling for many readers.

The Road Ahead

This book was written to guide you through the Olivet Discourse and Jesus' teaching about the future in all four Gospels. In focusing on what Jesus taught regarding the future, we won't consider passages in which Jesus predicted his own death and resurrection or passages that speak about the kingdom of God as a present reality. These, of course, are important topics but would distract from our attention on Jesus and the future, that is, the period *following* Jesus' resurrection.

Part 1 walks through the Olivet Discourse step by step by looking at all three Synoptic Gospels jointly. This parallel reading of the Olivet Discourse is one of the chief contributions of this book. Most commentaries and studies focus on one of the Gospels. Of the three, Mark is

---

10. Other reasons will be discussed in Part 1 below.
11. See, for example, 1 Corinthians 15.

normally given most attention because many believe it was the first Gospel written. In this vein, Matthew and Luke are viewed as interpretations of Mark. This approach often marginalizes the reality that Matthew and Luke also had access to eyewitness testimony and oral reports that were independent from Mark. Paul's reference to Jesus' Olivet Discourse in 1 Thessalonians 4:15–16 was most likely written even before the Gospel of Mark, which shows that the Olivet Discourse and Jesus' teaching about the end times were well known and widely discussed in the early church even before Mark wrote his Gospel, most likely on the basis of Peter's preaching.

Part 2 explores four main topics that cover all of Jesus' teaching about the future. These broader topics are (1) future persecution, (2) the growing conflict that would lead to the destruction of Jerusalem, (3) the need for patient waiting for Jesus' return and the unspecified period of time preceding the coming of the Son of Man, and (4) the events surrounding the end—resurrection, judgment, reward, and punishment.

The goal of this study is to equip you to evaluate the various approaches to interpreting the Olivet Discourse and determine for yourself which one best fits the biblical evidence. This book focuses on a proper understanding of Jesus' teaching about the future, but it is not just a matter of information. It is our hope that such a proper understanding will change you spiritually. Few passages in the Bible were written just to inform the intellectually curious. We're *in*formed to be *trans*formed. We'll therefore conclude the book by reflecting on how Jesus' teaching about the future was intended to impact, challenge, and transform us in the way we live our lives.

Finally, Appendix 1 examines the language of cosmic upheaval in the Hebrew prophets. This background provides important evidence for our understanding of Jesus' description of cosmic upheaval in his teaching about the future. Appendix 2 provides summary charts concerning Jesus' teaching about the future.

While based on thorough and prolonged study, this is not primarily an academic book, so there is no attempt to address every possible interpretive option. Our goal is not to write a scholarly monograph but to help interested readers understand Jesus' teaching about the future in the Gospels. In addition, you are certainly encouraged to further engage the sources cited in the footnotes. Instead of interacting with every conceivable interpretation, we'll aim to provide you with a clear discussion of what Jesus taught about the future in the hope that you'll have the information you need to arrive at your own informed decision regarding what Jesus taught about the end times and the events surrounding his return.

Jesus' Major Discourse about the Future: The Olivet Discourse

Introduction to Part 1

The Olivet Discourse is the foundation for understanding what Jesus taught about the future, so it is the best place to begin our study. As noted in the introduction, Jesus was widely viewed by his contemporaries as a prophet and, unlike many modern prophets who keep their prophecies vague to avoid falsification, Jesus wasn't afraid to predict specifically both near and far future events. Although we'll indicate our position in the discussion below, we hope to provide you with enough information to make your own informed interpretive decision concerning the meaning of Jesus' teaching about the future.

Before looking at the Olivet Discourse, it'll be important to understand how the accounts in Matthew, Mark, and Luke relate to each other and to the historical Jesus. These accounts are quite similar and often treated jointly as the "Synoptic Gospels." The term "synoptic" means "to see together, to have the same view or outlook," suggesting that these three Gospels present a rather similar picture of Jesus' life and teachings. Nevertheless, the Synoptics are quite distinct in wording, content, and order.[1] John's Gospel is also all about Jesus but for the most part features additional stories and teachings.

---

1. Andreas J. Köstenberger, L. Scott Kellum, and Charles L. Quarles, *The Cradle, the Cross, and the Crown: An Introduction to the New Testament*, 2nd ed. (Nashville: B & H Academic, 2016), 175–77.

Most historians and biblical scholars think that Mark's Gospel was written first, and the earliest Christian traditions connect Mark with Peter's preaching in Rome in the early 60s.[2] Matthew and Luke subsequently wrote their Gospels with knowledge of Mark in addition to their own experience and knowledge of Jesus. Others believe Matthew wrote first and Mark and Luke both wrote their Gospels in dialogue with and dependence on Matthew. We don't need to go into details here other than to point out that there is broad consensus that Luke was not written first and that he had access to Matthew, Mark, or both. This is significant because as we study the Olivet Discourse, we'll often find that Luke clarifies what might otherwise be difficult to understand in Matthew and Mark, particularly regarding the "abomination of desolation."

The reason for a parallel or synoptic reading of these three Gospels is to derive the maximum benefit from studying them together. Each evangelist was associated with Jesus or with an original eyewitness and wrote to preserve the memory of the teachings and actions of Jesus to strengthen the first-century churches and convince unbelievers of the reality of what God had accomplished in Jesus. Each Gospel contains unique stories and teachings, and in the case of overlap, the Gospels often provide different details and perspectives. The Gospel writers recorded what Jesus said and did, but their accounts are not video or audio recordings; they are written narratives. Because of this, each Gospel writer chose different stories to include and different details to highlight based on what they thought was important for fellow believers to know. They included some of their own comments to clarify difficult material and often arranged accounts topically rather than chronologically. Authorial selectivity explains most of the differences between the Gospels and provides a rich resource for us today. Reading the four different inspired accounts together gives us a fuller picture of what Jesus taught about the future and of how the earliest Christians understood and passed down his teaching to future generations.

The four chapters in Part 1 will lead you through an inductive study of Jesus' Olivet Discourse section by section. We'll provide the text of Matthew, Mark, and Luke in parallel columns so that you can compare the Gospels for yourself at each point.

---

2. See, for example, 1 Peter 5:13.

Chapter 1

Jesus' Prophecy and the Disciples' Questions

Matthew 24:1–2	Mark 13:1–2	Luke 21:5–6
Jesus left the temple and was going away, when his disciples came to point out to him *the buildings of the temple.*	And as he came out of the temple, one of his disciples said to him, *"Look, Teacher, what wonderful stones and what wonderful buildings!"*	And while some were speaking of the temple, how it was adorned with noble stones and offerings, he said,
² But he answered them, "You see all these, do you not? Truly, I say to you, there will not be left here one stone upon another that will not be thrown down.	² And Jesus said to him, "Do you see these great buildings? There will not be left here one stone upon another that will not be thrown down."	"As for these things that you see, the days will come when there will not be left here one stone upon another that will not be thrown down."

The Olivet Discourse begins with a dramatic prophecy: The temple will be destroyed. The disciples were shocked, perplexed, and concerned and asked Jesus the question that would have been on our minds if we had been there: When would this momentous event take place? Jesus' prophecy about the destruction of the temple and the disciples' questions jumpstart the Olivet Discourse.

Jesus' Prophecy

Both Matthew and Mark note that the conversation began between the disciples and Jesus as they were leaving the temple. Herod the Great's rebuilding and restoration of the Jerusalem temple had transformed it into one of the wonders of the ancient world. The disciples' admiration would have been similarly expressed by any Greek, Roman, or Jewish visitor to the temple. The disciples' amazement is shared even by modern visitors who see the huge blocks in the remaining Herodian walls, and these were only the substructure, not the temple proper. Herod was quite famous for a provincial client king at the time, and the temple dramatically increased Greek and Roman tourism, particularly because it was built in such a way that non-Jews had partial access through the court of Gentiles.

Josephus, the most important Jewish historian of the first century, described the beauty and magnificence of the temple in these words:

> The exterior of the building wanted nothing that could astound either mind or eye. For, being covered on all sides with massive plates of gold, the sun was no sooner up than it radiated so fiery a flash that persons straining to look at it were compelled to avert their eyes, as from the solar rays. To approaching strangers, it appeared from a distance like a snow-clad mountain; for all that was not overlaid with gold was of purest white. From its summit protruded sharp golden spikes to prevent birds from settling upon and polluting the roof. Some of the stones in the building were forty-five cubits in length, five in height and six in breadth.[1]

The Jerusalem temple was a magnificent sight and an astounding architectural achievement: "Easily the tallest structure in the city, it dominated the urban landscape. At about 1,550,000 square feet (thirty-five acres), it was also the largest sanctuary site in the ancient world."[2]

---

1. Josephus, *The Jewish War*, trans. H. ST. J. Thackeray, LCL 210 (Cambridge, MA: Harvard University Press, 1928, 1990), 5.222–24. All quotations from Josephus come from the Loeb Classical Library.
2. Adam Kolman Marshak, *The Many Faces of Herod the Great* (Grand Rapids: Eerdmans, 2015), 316.

The religious importance of the temple for the Jewish people cannot be overestimated. This was the place where worship took place and God could be entreated. This was the ultimate symbol of God's election of the Jewish people and of his commitment and promises to them: "The temple was thus regarded as the place where YHWH lived and ruled in the midst of Israel, and where, through the sacrificial system which reached its climax in the great festivals, he lived in grace, forgiving them, restoring them, and enabling them to be cleansed of defilement and so to continue as his people."[3]

Jesus' departure from the temple represents the end of his teaching ministry in Jerusalem. It is possible that this departure symbolizes judgment and the temple's abandonment by God in the same way that the glory of God left the temple and came to rest on the mountain east of the city in Ezekiel's vision (10:18–19; 11:22–23), but neither Matthew nor Mark make this explicit while Luke doesn't mention Jesus' departure at all.[4]

The disciples would have been shocked by Jesus' prophetic response. In reply to their awe at the temple's grandeur, Jesus prophesied that it would be razed to the ground. Jesus' prophecy of the temple's destruction would have made a profound impact on his Jewish listeners, many of whom viewed the temple as indestructible. During Jesus' trial later that week, false witnesses distorted this prophecy and claimed that Jesus had personally threatened to destroy the temple (Matt. 26:61; 27:40). This is reminiscent of the way in which King Jehoiakim had the prophet Uriah killed for prophesying the destruction of Jerusalem (Jer. 26:20–23) and Jewish priests and prophets wanted Jeremiah killed for prophesying against the city (Jer. 26:11).

Jesus' prophecy of the temple's destruction was used at his trial to support the death sentence. This charge continued to linger after Jesus' death and was also leveled against Stephen, one of his followers (Acts 6:13–14). For some Jews, Jesus' prophecy of the temple's destruction was enough to discredit him and his followers in subsequent generations. Jesus' original

---

3. N. T. Wright, *The New Testament and the People of God*, Christian Origins and the Question of God (Minneapolis: Fortress, 1992), 224–25.

4. For arguments that Jesus' departure from the temple is significant as a foreshadowing of future judgment see R. T. France, *The Gospel of Mark: A Commentary on the Greek Text* (Grand Rapids: Eerdmans, 2002), 495.

listeners, of course, would have been familiar with Old Testament prophecies of the destruction of Solomon's temple that had occurred in 586 BC, but they wouldn't have viewed the current temple as susceptible to such judgment (Jer. 7:11–14; 26:1–23; Micah 3:12).

The statement that not "one stone" would be left "upon another" indicates utter destruction that reverses the building process (Hag. 2:15). Some stones still rest upon another from the substructure and retaining wall of the temple Mount (the Wailing Wall), so Jesus was either referring to the temple buildings or was using prophetic hyperbole to stress the reality of total and irreversible destruction. His prophetic statement receives extra weight by the phrase "Truly, I say to you," which prefaces it in Matthew's Gospel. Jesus' statement is emphatic and final: The temple is going to be destroyed.

This prophecy is significant for at least three reasons. First, by predicting the temple's demise Jesus made clear to his disciples that he was fully aware of what lay ahead. His power to predict the future was also evident in his foreknowledge of Judas's betrayal and Peter's denial. Jesus was not merely guessing, and he certainly didn't simply prophesy things people were itching to hear. He was a genuine prophet; in fact, he was "the" prophet of whom Moses spoke:

> The LORD your God will raise up for you a prophet like me from among you, from your brothers—it is to him you shall listen— just as you desired of the LORD your God at Horeb on the day of the assembly, when you said, "Let me not hear again the voice of the LORD my God or see this great fire any more, lest I die." And the LORD said to me, "They are right in what they have spoken. I will raise up for them a prophet like you from among their brothers. And I will put my words in his mouth, and he shall speak to them all that I command him. And whoever will not listen to my words that he shall speak in my name, I myself will require it of him." (Deut. 18:15–18)

Second, the fact that no Gospel writer mentions the fulfillment of this prophecy suggests that these accounts were written before Jerusalem fell and the temple was destroyed by the Romans in AD 70. If any of them had known about the prophecy's fulfillment, he would surely have commented on it. The Gospel writers weren't making up prophecies after the fact (*vaticinia ex eventu*) but recording a legitimate prophecy uttered before the events transpired.[5]

Third, and perhaps most importantly, this prophecy sets the stage for the entire Olivet Discourse. Any interpretation of Matthew 24, Mark 13, and Luke 21 that doesn't relate in some way to the historical destruction of the temple is on the wrong track. This prophecy sets the topic for the discourse. This doesn't mean that Jesus couldn't talk about other things beyond the destruction of Jerusalem in the Olivet Discourse, but this event is surely the starting point as we seek to understand what else Jesus might have said about the future.

The Disciples' Questions

Matthew 24:3	Mark 13:3–4	Luke 21:7
[3] As he sat on the Mount of Olives, the disciples came to him privately, saying, "Tell us, when will these things be, and what will be the sign of your coming and of the end of the age?"	[3] And as he sat on the Mount of Olives opposite the temple, Peter and James and John and Andrew asked him privately, [4] *"Tell us, when will these things be, and what will be the sign when all these things are about to be accomplished?"*	[7] And they asked him, "Teacher, when will these things be, and what will be the sign when these things are about to take place?"

Luke doesn't comment on the location, but Matthew and Mark indicate that Jesus and his followers had moved to the Mount of Olives, about halfway to where they were spending the night in Bethany. During the walk, the disciples were probably still processing the shock of Jesus' prophecy and couldn't wait to ask for more details. Jesus had made clear that the temple would be destroyed but didn't specify the time or sign that would precede its destruction. This naturally led to the questions posed by the

---

5. See Bo Reicke, "Synoptic Prophecies on the Destruction of Jerusalem," in *Studies in New Testament and Early Christian Literature: Essays in Honor of Allen P. Wikgren*, ed. David E. Aune (Leiden: Brill, 1972), 121–34.

disciples: When would these things happen? What sign would indicate that they were about to take place? In Mark and Luke, the disciples' dual question doesn't seem to go beyond Jesus' prophecy about the temple's destruction.[6] They wanted to know when it would take place and what sign would precede the catastrophe.

However, the way in which the question is expanded in Matthew's account seems to point beyond the destruction of the temple toward Jesus' second coming. In Matthew, the disciples ask: "Tell us, when will these things be [the destruction of the temple as in Mark and Luke], and what will be the sign of your coming *and of the end of the age?*"

N. T. Wright focuses on the original historical situation to argue that it wouldn't have made sense for Jesus to talk about his second coming while still with the disciples and that the reference to his "coming" refers to Jesus' coming to Jerusalem to reign as King.[7] However, it is likely that the disciples would have understood the temple's demise as a cataclysmic event that would take place only at the end of the present evil age and the dawning of the promised age to come. They would have thought of one, not two, events separated by thousands of years, so from the perspective of the original disciples the question in Matthew is the same as that in Mark and Luke.

Wright's interpretation of the disciples' question in Matthew is possible, and we will consider it in chapter 3. For now, it will suffice to note that many interpreters think that Matthew is in fact distinguishing two separate events with his expanded question. First, when will these things take place (i.e., when will the temple be destroyed?). Second, what will be the sign of Jesus' second coming and of the end of the age? If this is correct, it suggests that Jesus in the Olivet Discourse is discussing two distinct historical events separated from each other by a certain amount of time. This is rendered more likely in Matthew by the additional material he features

---

6. Robert H. Stein argues that "these things" and "all these things" refer to the destruction of the temple. He notes, "Of the twenty-six instances in which the expression 'all these things' (*tauta panta*) occurs in the New Testament, twenty-four of them have its referent occurring before the expression" (*Jesus, the Temple, and the Coming Son of Man: A Commentary on Mark 13* [Downers Grove, IL: IVP Academic, 2014], 68). He also notes how Mark often uses dual or multiple questions with the same referent (7:18; 8:17–18; 9:19; 11:28; 14:37).

7. N. T. Wright, *Jesus and the Victory of God* (Minneapolis: Fortress, 1996), 345.

at the end of his version of the discourse that is not included in Mark and Luke (most of Matt. 24:37–25:46). This unique Matthean material pertains to the future second coming.

The Main Interpretive Question

The question to keep in mind as we move forward is bound up with these two main events: *When is Jesus prophesying about the destruction of Jerusalem and the temple by the Romans in the year 70, and when is he prophesying about his second coming and the full establishment of his kingdom?* The initial question asked by the disciples focused on the timing of the destruction of the temple, so it would make sense for Jesus to begin by responding to that question first.

Chapter 2

Possible Signs, the Abomination of Desolation, and the Destruction of the City

In the previous chapter, we looked at the dialogue that triggered the Olivet Discourse. Jesus predicted that the Jerusalem temple would be destroyed and the disciples responded by inquiring about the timing of this destructive judgment (Matthew, Mark, and Luke) and about Jesus' return (Matthew only). It is our conviction that Jesus did answer the disciples' question about the timing of the destruction of the temple. He didn't just ignore their question and begin talking about events that would happen thousands of years later. They wanted—even needed—to know when the temple would be destroyed. The temple was the center of Judaism, the center of their hope, and the center of their world. Jesus' prediction of the temple's destruction would have been one of the most startling, controversial, and earthshattering claims of his entire teaching ministry, perhaps only rivaled by the proclamation that the kingdom of God had come near. It would be foolish for modern readers to treat the Olivet Discourse as if it had nothing to do with Jesus' prophecy of the temple's destruction. The challenge, however, is discerning when he is speaking about the destruction of the year 70 and when he is talking about his future coming to establish God's kingdom on earth.

As we work through this chapter, we'll see that everything in Mark 13:5–23 (along with parallels in Matthew and Luke) makes good sense as Jesus' description of the time before, during, and immediately after the destruction of Jerusalem in the year 70. Luke's account is the clearest in this regard and will provide crucial guidance in helping us separate Jesus' teaching about the destruction of Jerusalem in the immediate future from that regarding his future coming in the distant future. In the next chapter, we'll look at Jesus' teaching in the Olivet Discourse about his second coming.

Possible Signs Preceding the End: Palestine

Matt 24:4–8	Mark 13:5–8	Luke 21:8–11
[4] And Jesus answered them, "See that no one leads you astray. [5] For many will come in my name, saying, 'I am the Christ,' and they will lead many astray. [6] And you will hear of wars and rumors of wars. See that you are not alarmed, for this must take place, *but the end is not yet.*	[5] And Jesus began to say to them, "See that no one leads you astray. [6] Many will come in my name, saying, 'I am he!' and they will lead many astray. [7] And when you hear of wars and rumors of wars, do not be alarmed. This must take place, *but the end is not yet.*	[8] And he said, "See that you are not led astray. For many will come in my name, saying, 'I am he!' and, 'The time is at hand!' Do not go after them. [9] And when you hear of wars and tumults, do not be terrified, for these things must first take place, *but the end will not be at once."*
[7] For nation will rise against nation, and kingdom against kingdom, and there will be famines and earthquakes in various places. [8] All these are but the beginning of the birth pains."	[8] For nation will rise against nation, and kingdom against kingdom. There will be earthquakes in various places; there will be famines. These are but the beginning of the birth pains."	

Jesus began his answer to the disciples' question concerning the timing of the destruction of Jerusalem and the end of the age by giving a series of non-signs. These are persons or events (false messiahs, wars, famines, and earthquakes) that will appear or take place but won't indicate that the end is near and won't constitute the sign for which they were asking. It's interesting that even though many think these verses describe signs prior to the end, Jesus explicitly warned the disciples against being deceived, cautioning them that these things don't yet constitute the end. They mark only the beginning of "birth pains." The metaphor of birth pains may indicate that these things will increase in intensity as time goes on, though this isn't explicitly stated.

Yet what "end" is in view: the destruction of Jerusalem and the temple or Jesus' second coming? At this point, it's not necessary to distinguish between the two since Jesus isn't listing signs of the end but rather persons or events that could trouble or confuse his followers but were just an ordinary part of unfolding history. They are not signs of the end, and his followers must be on guard not to be deceived and think that these things are signaling the end. Even as these things have been evident through history, they were all also fulfilled between the years 30 and 70, so the non-signs don't necessarily point beyond the cataclysmic events of the year 70.

First, Jesus warned that some would claim to be the *Messiah* and deceive many. It's not that these people would claim to be *Jesus* but that they would claim to be the *true Jewish Messiah*. If a Christian were to follow one of these false messianic claimants, it would involve a rejection of trust in *Jesus* as Messiah. Any followers of these false messiahs would also share their fate.

Messianic Pretenders: AD 30–70*

1. *An unnamed Samaritan* (AD 36): "The Samaritan nation too was not exempt from disturbance. For a man . . . rallied them, bidding them go in a body with him to Mount Gerizim, which in their belief is the most sacred of mountains. . . . But before they could ascend, Pilate blocked their projected route up the mountain with a detachment of cavalry and heavy-armed infantry. . . . Many prisoners were taken, of whom Pilate put to death the principal leaders and those who were most influential among the fugitives" (Josephus, *Antiquities* 18.85–87).

2. *Theudas* (AD 44–46): "During the period when Fadus was procurator of Judaea, a certain imposter named Theudas persuaded the majority of the masses to take up their possessions and to follow him to the Jordan River. He stated that he was a prophet and that at his command the river would be parted and would provide them an

easy passage. With this talk he deceived many. Fadus, however, did not permit them to reap the fruit of their folly, but sent against them unexpectedly, slew many of them and took many prisoners. Theudas himself was captured, whereupon they cut off his head and brought it to Jerusalem" (Josephus, *Antiquities* 20.97–99; cf. Acts 5:36).

3. *Unnamed imposters* (AD 52–58): "In Judaea matters were constantly going from bad to worse. For the country was again infested with bands of brigands and imposters who deceived the mob. Not a day passed, however, but that Felix captured and put to death many of these imposters and brigands" (Josephus, *Antiquities* 20.160–61).

4. *Other unnamed imposters* (AD 52–58): "Moreover, imposters and deceivers called upon the mob to follow them into the desert. For they said that they would show them unmistakable marvels and signs that would be wrought in harmony with God's design. Many were, in fact, persuaded and paid the penalty for their folly; for they were brought before Felix and he punished them" (Josephus, *Antiquities* 20.167–68).

5. *The Egyptian* (AD 52–58): "At this time there came to Jerusalem from Egypt a man who declared that he was a prophet and advised the masses of the common people to go out with him to the mountain called the Mount of Olives, which lies opposite the city at a distance of five furlongs. For he asserted that he wished to demonstrate from there that at his command Jerusalem's walls would fall down, through which he promised to provide them an entrance into the city. When Felix heard of this he ordered his soldiers to take up their arms. Setting out from Jerusalem with a large force of cavalry and infantry, he fell upon the Egyptian and his followers, slaying four hundred of them and taking two hundred prisoners. The Egyptian himself escaped from the battle and disappeared" (Josephus, *Antiquities* 20.169–72; cf. Acts 21:38).

6. *Another unnamed imposter* (AD 59–62): "Festus also sent a force of cavalry and infantry against the dupes of a certain imposter who had promised them salvation and rest from troubles, if they chose to follow him into the wilderness. The force which Festus dispatched

destroyed both the deceiver himself and those who had followed him" (Josephus, *Antiquities* 20.188).

7. *Leaders of the Jewish Revolt* (AD 66–70): Several leaders of the Jewish revolt likely presented themselves as messianic figures. Menahem raided Masada for weapons and "returned like a veritable king to Jerusalem" (Josephus, *Jewish War* 2.434). John of Gischala acted like a tyrant (*Jewish War* 2.585–89; 4.121–27). And Simon bar-Giora changed the coinage from "The Freedom of Zion" to read "The Redemption of Zion," indicating a probable messianic aspect to his propaganda and self-presentation (*Jewish War* 4.503–83; 7.26–32).

8. *Vespasian* (AD 70): Although Vespasian did not claim messiah-ship for himself, Josephus presented him in such terms: "But what more than all else incited them to the war was an ambiguous oracle, likewise found in their sacred scriptures [Num.24:17–19?], to the effect that at that time one from their country would become ruler of the world. This they understood to mean someone of their own race, and many of their wise men went astray in their interpretation of it. The oracle, however, in reality signified the sovereignty of Vespasian, who was proclaimed Emperor on Jewish soil" (Josephus, *Jewish War* 6.312–13; cf. Suetonius, *Life of Vespasian* 4.5; Tacitus, *Histories* 5.13).

---

* Josephus doesn't indicate that any of these imposters explicitly claimed to be the messiah but they certainly acted with what could be described as messianic aspirations, and the fact that Josephus doesn't use the actual term "messiah" doesn't mean that some or all these figures didn't present themselves as such. Messianic pretenders between AD 6 and 30 include Judas the Galilean, Simon the Peraean, and Athronges the Judean (*Antiquities* 17.271–85; *Jewish War* 2.56–65).

Second, Jesus warned of *wars* and *rumors of wars*. In the 30s and early 60s there were disturbances and conflicts with the Parthian empire to the East. The Parthians were a long-standing threat to Rome, and Palestine was a buffer and pawn throughout the long conflict. Apart from the Parthians, there was constant unrest within Palestine itself. Finally, the Jewish revolt against the Romans began in the year 66. Apart from actual fighting, there would have been constant rumors of war during the years 30–70.

Third, *famine* was a constant threat in the ancient world, and first-century Roman emperors often minted coins featuring Ceres (the goddess of agriculture and grain crops) and Annona (the goddess of grain supply) as imperial propaganda to assure citizens that the emperor could guarantee a steady supply of food. The emperors were primarily concerned with the supply of grain to the city of Rome and to the legions, and the provinces often had to fend for themselves as best they could. Josephus describes a terrible famine that took place in the years 46 to 48: "It was in the administration of Tiberius Alexander that the great famine occurred in Judaea, during which Queen Helena bought grain from Egypt for large sums and distributed it to the needy" (Josephus, *Antiquities* 20.101; cf. *Antiquities* 3.320; 20.51–53). This was a significant famine, and Luke described how Agabus prophesied about it with the result that the church in Antioch raised support and sent it to the Judean Christians through Barnabas and Saul (Acts 11:28–30).

Fourth, Jesus prophesied that there would be *earthquakes*. Earthquakes were known in the ancient world but were not scientifically understood and often caused considerable alarm. Josephus describes an earthquake that took place during the Jewish War of the years 66–70:

> For in the course of the night a terrific storm broke out: the winds blew a hurricane, rain fell in torrents, lightning was continuous, accompanied by fearful thunder-caps and extraordinary rumblings of earthquake. Such convulsion of the very fabric of the universe clearly foretokened destruction for mankind, and the conjecture was natural that these were portents of no trifling calamity. In this the Idumaeans and the city folk were of one mind: the former being persuaded that God was wroth at their expedition and that they were not to escape retribution for bearing arms against the metropolis, Ananus and his party believing that they had won the day without a contest and that God was directing the battle on their behalf. (Josephus, *Jewish War* 4.286–88)

According to Josephus, many interpreted the cosmic upheaval (storm, wind, lightning, thunder, earthquake) as a sign of impending doom, while some of the defenders interpreted it as a sign that God would destroy their enemies.

It is important to keep in mind that Jesus didn't list these things—false messiahs, wars, famines, earthquakes—so that his followers could know that the end was near but that they wouldn't be unduly concerned or alarmed by the occurrence of these things. They weren't signs of the end, and Jesus distanced these ordinary but destructive events of human history from "the end." In the Old Testament, the metaphor of "birth pains" is often connected with the destruction of a city, so "end" here likely relates to the destruction of Jerusalem and the temple in the year 70.[1]

Possible Signs of the End: The Christian Community

Matthew 24:9–14	Mark 13:9–13	Luke 21:12–19	Parallel Passage: Matthew 10:17–22 [Jesus' earlier instructions to his disciples]
9 "Then they will deliver you up to tribulation and put you to death, and you will be hated by all nations for my name's sake. 10 And then many will fall away and betray one another and hate one another.	9 "But be on your guard. For they will deliver you over to councils, and you will be beaten in synagogues, and you will stand before governors and kings for my sake, to bear witness before them. 10 And the gospel must first be proclaimed to all nations.	12 But *before all this* they will lay their hands on you and persecute you, delivering you up to the synagogues and prisons, and you will be brought before kings and governors for my name's sake. 13 This will be your opportunity to bear witness. 14 Settle it therefore in your minds not to meditate beforehand how to answer,	17 Beware of men, for they will deliver you over to courts and flog you in their synagogues, 18 and you will be dragged before governors and kings for my sake, to bear witness before them and the Gentiles.

---

1. Isaiah 13:8; 21:3; 26:17; Jeremiah 4:31; 6:24; 22:23; 30:6; 50:43; Hosea 13:13; Micah 4:9–10.

Matthew 24:9–14	Mark 13:9–13	Luke 21:12–19	Parallel Passage: Matthew 10:17–22
[11] And many false prophets will arise and lead many astray. [12] And because lawlessness will be increased, the love of many will grow cold. [13] But the one who endures to the *end* will be saved. [14] And this gospel of the kingdom will be proclaimed throughout the whole world as a testimony to all nations, and then the *end* will come.	[11] And when they bring you to trial and deliver you over, do not be anxious beforehand what you are to say, but say whatever is given you in that hour, for it is not you who speak, but the Holy Spirit. [12] And brother will deliver brother over to death, and the father his child, and children will rise against parents and have them put to death. [13] And you will be hated by all for my name's sake. But the one who endures to the *end* will be saved.	[15] for I will give you a mouth and wisdom, which none of your adversaries will be able to withstand or contradict. [16] You will be delivered up even by parents and brothers and relatives and friends, and some of you they will put to death. [17] You will be hated by all for my name's sake. [18] But not a hair of your head will perish. [19] By your endurance you will gain your lives [or "souls"].	[19] When they deliver you over, do not be anxious how you are to speak or what you are to say, for what you are to say will be given to you in that hour. [20] For it is not you who speak, but the Spirit of your Father speaking through you. [21] Brother will deliver brother over to death, and the father his child, and children will rise against parents and have them put to death, [22] and you will be hated by all for my name's sake. But the one who endures to the *end* will be saved.

The first signs mentioned by Jesus as non-indicators of the end applied to Christians and non-Christians alike. Everyone in Palestine would encounter false messiahs, wars, rumors of wars, famines, and earthquakes. In this section of the Olivet Discourse, Jesus switches focus a little and gives specific instructions to his followers regarding the future. They will be persecuted, beaten, thrown in prison, and killed. There will be betrayal and hatred, the love of many will grow cold, and his followers must be on guard against false prophets. If they endure faithfully, they'll be saved. Finally, the good news of Jesus' kingdom will be proclaimed throughout the whole inhabited world. Luke adds an important remark concerning timing when he notes that this persecution will begin "before all this," a reference to the coming of false messiahs and wars. Persecution will begin immediately. The parallel Matthew 10:17–22 is found much earlier in Matthew's Gospel and indicates that Jesus had previously discussed these things with his disciples; it is likely that he taught on these matters on more than one occasion.

This section of the Olivet Discourse deals mainly with coming persecution. The New Testament writers repeatedly warn believers about persecution, betrayal, and the danger of falling away from the faith.[2] Perseverance or apostasy was the stark alternative in times of hardship and persecution in the early church.

Truth Touches Life: Persecution

Jesus was not a good salesman by the world's standards. He also wasn't particularly seeker-sensitive. He repeatedly warned his followers that they would suffer and face difficulty due to their allegiance to him. It was as if he were saying, "Come, follow me, but know that your life will get harder. Your friends may desert you. In fact, many will oppose you because of me." Salespersons focus primarily if not exclusively on benefits and generally try to minimize any potential problems or difficulties. Jesus was the opposite. He wanted his followers to be fully aware of the challenges they would encounter. He wanted them to enter a relationship with him with their eyes wide open.

Why follow Jesus if this will lead to increased difficulties, opposition, and persecution? In the world's eyes, this is a fair question. In short, the answer is: Because his message is true. Because he is who he claimed to be. Because he is the world's rightful and true ruler and there will be a future judgment.

---

2. 2 Thessalonians 2:3; 1 Timothy 4:1–3; 2 Timothy 3:1–9; 2 Peter 3:3; 1 John 2:18–19; Revelation 13:12–17.

Because he promised his presence and peace amid the intense suffering he knew we would encounter. All the prosperity, success, money, and power in the world cannot produce love, joy, or peace; the most important and valuable things in life can't be bought and are available only in and through a relationship with Jesus Christ.

The book of Acts recounts how Jesus' words here were fulfilled very quickly. The earliest Christians almost immediately began to face persecution, imprisonment, false prophets, division, death (Stephen and James), and trials before the Jewish council, synagogues, Roman government officials, and kings.[3] Jesus prepared his followers that they would face these difficulties because of him (Matt. 24:9; Mark 13:9; Luke 21:17). Their allegiance to Jesus wouldn't make their lives easier or lead to prosperity but would lead to just the opposite. Such opposition wouldn't be an indication of God's judgment but of their faithfulness. Comfort could be found in the fact that they wouldn't be alone in defending themselves and all this opposition would provide opportunities to witness. Acts 4:13–14 is an example of this Spirit-empowered witness as the religious leaders are astonished at the boldness of Peter and John even though they were "uneducated, common men." Jesus connected this Spirit-empowered witness with the proclamation of the gospel to all nations.

Two things need further attention. First, all three Synoptic Gospels stress the need for faithful endurance and connect this endurance with salvation (Luke speaks of "gaining your souls"). It is possible that this salvation conveys simple survival but this is unlikely since some believers would die as they endured (Luke 21:16: "and some of you they will put to death"). Jesus is instead connecting this promise of salvation with the way the term is more commonly understood throughout the New Testament, a favorable verdict at the last judgment and entrance into the new heavens

---

3. Acts 4:1–22; 5:1–11, 17–42; 6:1–8:3; 9:1–2, 13–16, 23–24; 12:1–19; 13:44, 50; 14:4–7, 19–20; 15:1–2; 16:19–40; 17:5–9, 13, 32; 18:12–17; 19:9, 23–41; 21:27–36; 22:22–26:32.

and new earth.[4] Significantly, Jesus doesn't link this salvation with a past event of conversion but rather with the present endurance of all the opposition his followers would encounter.

Second, Jesus provided a clear statement of what would precede the end: The gospel would be proclaimed to all nations. This brings us back to the question of what "end" is in view in this passage. "End" is not a technical term and in the Olivet Discourse could refer either to the destruction of Jerusalem and the temple in the year 70, the second coming and final judgment, or the end of an individual's life. Each reference to "end" must be assessed within its immediate context. Everything else Jesus has mentioned up to this point in the Olivet Discourse was both fulfilled during the period between the years 30–70 (false messiahs, wars, famines, earthquakes, persecutions, false prophets, imprisonments) and has occurred throughout the past 2,000 years of human history.

Some interpreters connect this end exclusively with the destruction of Jerusalem in the year 70 because Jesus' first hearers would have understood the "whole world" and "all nations" as the known world at the time (Rome and the nations at its borders), and the gospel was proclaimed throughout the inhabited world within the first generation of Christians.[5] Paul celebrated the fact that the mystery of the gospel had been made known to "all nations" (Rom. 16:26) and that the gospel was bearing fruit and growing in the "whole world" (Col. 1:6). On this reading, the gospel was proclaimed to all the nations in the whole known world before the temple was destroyed in the year 70. These are valid points since nothing thus far in the Olivet Discourse has indicated that Jesus has shifted from answering the question of when the temple would be destroyed to answering the question of his coming and the end of the age.

The more traditional interpretation is that the gospel must be proclaimed in the whole world to all the nations before the ultimate end, that is, before Jesus' return and the final resurrection and judgment. It is possible that end here is referring to the end of the age, but the context— Jesus' response to the disciples' question about the temple—suggests the

---

4. Craig S. Keener, *Matthew*, IVP New Testament Commentary (Downers Grove, IL: InterVarsity Press, 1997), 345–46.

5. Stein, *Jesus, the Temple, and the Coming Son of Man*, 83; R. T. France, *The Gospel of Matthew*, NICNT (Grand Rapids: Eerdmans), 909.

nearer timeframe of the year 70. There may be some intentional ambiguity since everything mentioned up to this point in the Olivet Discourse was both fulfilled by the year 70 yet has also characterized the last 2,000 years of history. In whichever way one interprets the end in Matthew 24:14, the missionary focus of the New Testament is strong and pervasive: the gospel of Jesus' kingdom must be proclaimed throughout the entire world.[6]

Truth Touches Life: Your Role in God's Kingdom

One of the gravest and most damaging misconceptions in the history of the church is that it is up to professional ministers to do the work of the ministry. This paralyzing mindset thinks that full-time pastors and missionaries will get the job done; evangelism and disciple-making are exclusively up to them. Yet nothing could be farther from the truth. To the contrary, every Christian has an essential role to play in God's kingdom.

We all have different skills, abilities, vocations, and circles of influence. We won't all make identical contributions but we're all supposed to play a role. Through the power of God's Spirit every Christian is God's representative and called to make a difference in this world, to proclaim the presence of the kingdom by both our words and our actions.

What role are you playing in the unfolding of history and the advance of God's kingdom? Don't compare yourself with others, and don't try to imitate others. Don't believe the lie that you have nothing to contribute. Ask God for wisdom and do everything your hand finds to do for his glory. No task is too insignificant, and no assignment too small to accomplish with excellence and distinction as unto the Lord.

---

6. See Matthew 28:18–20; Acts 1:8; Romans 10:14–15.

The Abomination of Desolation and
Destruction of the City

Matthew 24:15–22	Mark 13:14–20	Luke 21:20–24

Matthew 24:15–22

¹⁵ "So *when you see* the abomination of *desolation* spoken of by the prophet Daniel, standing in the holy place (let the reader understand), ¹⁶ then let those who are in Judea flee to the mountains. ¹⁷ Let the one who is on the housetop not go down to take what is in his house, ¹⁸ and let the one who is in the field not turn back to take his cloak. ¹⁹ And alas for women who are pregnant and for those who are nursing infants in those days! ²⁰ Pray that your flight may not be in winter or on a Sabbath. ²¹ For then there will be great tribulation, such as has not been from the beginning of the world until now, no, and never will be. ²² And if those days had not been cut short, no human being would be saved. But for the sake of the elect those days will be cut short."

Mark 13:14–20

¹⁴ "But *when you see* the abomination of *desolation* standing where he ought not to be (let the reader understand), then let those who are in Judea flee to the mountains. ¹⁵ Let the one who is on the housetop not go down, nor enter his house, to take anything out, ¹⁶ and let the one who is in the field not turn back to take his cloak. ¹⁷ And alas for women who are pregnant and for those who are nursing infants in those days! ¹⁸ Pray that it may not happen in winter. ¹⁹ For in those days there will be such tribulation as has not been from the beginning of the creation that God created until now, and never will be. ²⁰ And if the Lord had not cut short the days, no human being would be saved. But for the sake of the elect, whom he chose, he shortened the days."

Luke 21:20–24

²⁰ "But *when you see* Jerusalem surrounded by armies, then know that its *desolation* has come near. ²¹ Then let those who are in Judea flee to the mountains, and let those who are inside the city depart, and let not those who are out in the country enter it, ²² for these are days of vengeance, to fulfill all that is written. ²³ Alas for women who are pregnant and for those who are nursing infants in those days! For there will be great distress upon the earth and wrath against this people.

²⁴ They will fall by the edge of the sword and be led captive among all nations, and Jerusalem will be trampled underfoot by the Gentiles, until the times of the Gentiles are fulfilled."

With the abomination of desolation—or desolating sacrilege, depending on your translation—things get interesting, and many readers become needlessly confused. One simple guideline will help keep us on track:

Let Scripture interpret Scripture. It is here that our parallel reading of Matthew, Mark, and Luke will really begin to pay off. Especially Luke offers clear guidance on the meaning of the abomination of desolation.

At the beginning of the Olivet Discourse, the disciples asked *when* the temple would be destroyed (Matthew, Mark, Luke) and what would be the *sign* of its destruction (Mark and Luke). Up to this point in the Olivet Discourse, Jesus has not given a sign but rather has listed a series of events that will take place prior to the destruction of the temple. Now he focuses on one singular visible incident, the abomination of desolation; this likely is the sign for which the disciples were asking.[7]

Matthew makes clear that the abomination of desolation relates to the book of Daniel and relates to the desecration of the temple (the "Holy Place").[8] Many extensive and complex charts and theories have been developed to try to interpret Daniel's prophecies but ancient interpretations of Daniel are often ignored. Daniel's book was widely read and discussed by Palestinian Jews in the centuries leading up to Jesus' life. These ancient interpreters connected Daniel's prophecies of the abomination of desolation to an event that took place in 167 BC.

The Abomination of Desolation: Antiochus IV Epiphanes (167 BC)

1. "Now the *desolation* of the temple came about *in accordance with the prophecy of Daniel*, which had been made four hundred and eight years before; for he had revealed that the Macedonians would destroy it" (Josephus, *Antiquities* 12.322).

2. "Now on the fifteenth day of Chislev, in the one hundred forty-fifth year [167 BC] they erected a *desolating sacrilege* on the altar of burnt offering. . . . On the twenty-fifth day of the month they offered sacrifice on the altar that was on top of the altar of burnt offering" (1 Macc. 1:54, 59).*

3. "The king sent an Athenian senator to compel the Jews to forsake the laws of their ancestors and no longer to live by the laws of God;

---

7. Stein, *Jesus, the Temple, and the Coming Son of Man*, 87.
8. Daniel refers to the abomination of desolation in 8:13; 9:27; 11:31; and 12:11.

also to pollute the temple in Jerusalem and to call it the temple of Olympian Zeus" (2 Macc. 6:1–2a).

4. "Harsh and utterly grievous was the onslaught of evil. For the temple was filled with debauchery and reviling by the Gentiles, who dallied with prostitutes and had intercourse with women within the sacred precincts, and besides brought in things for sacrifice that were unfit. The altar was covered with *abominable* offerings that were forbidden by the laws" (2 Macc. 6:3–6).

5. "Not content with the unlooked for success in capturing the city and with the plunder and wholesale carnage, Antiochus . . . put pressure upon the Jews to violate the code of their country by leaving their infants uncircumcised and *sacrificing swine upon the altar*. These orders were disobeyed by all, and the most eminent defaulters were massacred" (Josephus, *Jewish War* 1.34–35).

6. "The king also built a pagan altar upon the temple-altar, and slaughtered swine thereon, thereby practicing a form of sacrifice neither lawful nor native to the religion of the Jews. And he compelled them to give up the worship of their own God, and to do reverence to the gods in whom he believed" (Josephus, *Antiquities* 12.253).

7. "Then Judas and his brothers . . . saw the sanctuary *desolate*, the altar profaned, and the gates burned" (1 Macc. 4:36, 38).

8. "Then someone came to him in Persia and reported . . . that they had torn down the *abomination* that he had erected on the altar in Jerusalem" (1 Macc. 6:7).

---

* All quotations from the Apocrypha are from Bruce Metzger and Roland Murphy, eds., *The New Oxford Annotated Apocrypha* (New York: Oxford University Press, 1991).

Antiochus IV Epiphanes erected an "abomination of desolation" in the Jerusalem temple as a part of his attempt to wipe out the Jewish faith. According to Josephus, this involved sacrificing pigs on the altar and dedicating the temple to Zeus. Judas Maccabees and his brothers recaptured and rededicated the temple in 164 BC, precisely three years after the abomination of desolation had been set up (1 Macc. 4:52–54; three and a half years after Antiochus had captured Jerusalem according to Josephus, *Jewish War* 1.19, 32–33). The Maccabees instituted the annual celebration called the "Festival of Lights" (*Hanukkah*) to commemorate the rededication of the temple. Jesus and his disciples would have celebrated this festival annually (John 10:22), and Jesus' mention of the abomination of desolation would have been connected at once to these events by his first hearers.

Jesus adopted this well-known language of "abomination of desolation" to prophesy a future similar ritual pollution of the temple. His reference to Daniel indicates that the desolation of 167 BC didn't complete the fulfillment of Daniel's prophecies. This could be understood in terms of double fulfillment or in terms of typology by which the earlier prophesied desecration of 167 BC was a type of the later more extensive and final desecration of the year 70. The comment by Matthew and Mark, "Let the reader understand," likely points to the continuity between Daniel, the abomination of desolation of 167 BC, and the future abomination of desolation: The temple would be ritually polluted.[9]

Although many interpretations have been proposed, there are two main but related possibilities with regard to the fulfillment of the abomination of desolation, the sign that the temple was about to be destroyed. First, the pollution of the temple by the Zealot defenders of Jerusalem around the years 67–68 is the fulfillment, perhaps involving the appointment of the unqualified Phanni as high priest (Josephus, *Jewish War* 4.147–57). This would have happened early enough to be a sign for Christians to flee before all possibility of escape was cut off. This is quite likely and related to the second possibility.

Second, Luke helpfully provides clarification for readers who may have been confused by the mention of the abomination of desolation in Matthew and Mark. When Luke wrote his Gospel, he had access to

---

9. Craig Evans argues that the occurrences of either "abomination" or "desolation" in the Greek translation of the Old Testament (the Septuagint, or LXX) refer to pagan worship or some form of idolatry (e.g., Deut. 29:17; 1 Kings 11:5, 7; 2 Kings 23:13, 24; Isa. 66:3; Jer. 4:1; 7:30; 13:27; 16:18; Ezek. 5:11; Zech. 9:7; 2 Chron. 15:8; Craig A. Evans, *Mark 8:27–16:20*, WBC 34B [Dallas: Word, 2002], 318). Jeremiah 7:30 states: "For the sons of Judah have done evil in my sight, declares the Lord. They have set their detestable things in the house that is called by my name, to defile it." Ezekiel 5:11 states: "because you have defiled my sanctuary with all your detestable things and with all your abominations, therefore I will withdraw. My eye will not spare, and I will have no pity."

Matthew, Mark, or both. Perceiving the possibility of confusion among his Gentile readers regarding the abomination of desolation, he clarified: "*When you see Jerusalem surrounded by armies*, then know that its desolation has come near" (Luke 21:20, emphasis added). He retains the key word "desolation" but tells us what Jesus meant by it: all that will transpire during the siege of Jerusalem by the Romans. The Roman siege itself didn't desecrate the temple (although Titus and the Romans certainly did once they got access to it in the year 70), but, as mentioned, the war against the Romans in Judea was well underway when the Zealots desecrated the temple.[10] Luke indicates that there will still be time to flee the city (21:21), so he has in mind the beginning of the advance of the Roman armies against Jerusalem before they had dug a trench and erected a wall around the city to cut off flight. Luke's insights must not be ignored at this point; he provides an early, canonical, and inspired description of what Jesus meant by "the abomination of desolation" in its original historical context.

The desecration of the temple by the Zealots and their pseudo-high priest and the approach of Roman armies were signs for Jesus' followers to flee from Judea without any delay to gather material possessions. Most of the inhabitants of Judea fled to Jerusalem for safety from the Roman armies, and according to Josephus, the city's population swelled to over one million people (*Jewish War* 6.420). In contrast, Jesus instructed his followers to leave the city and flee to the mountains. As with all situations involving displacement, it would be a particularly precarious time for pregnant and nursing mothers, which could be exacerbated by bad wintry weather. Matthew highlights the extra difficulty escape on the Sabbath would present for the Jewish Christians in Judea (24:20).

According to church tradition, the early Christians fled Jerusalem, not to the mountains, but to Pella in Perea.[11] The ancient church historian Eusebius (AD 260–340) reported the following:

---

10. According to Josephus, Titus and his generals walked into the sanctuary and viewed the "holy place of the sanctuary and all that it contained" (*Jewish War* 6.260). Later, the Roman soldiers sacrificed to their standards in the temple court (*Jewish War* 6.316).

11. This flight of the Jewish Christians is attested in Eusebius, *Ecclesiastical History* 3.5.3; Epiphanius, *Panarion or Refutation of Heresies* 29.7.7–8; 30.2.7; *Treatise on Weights and Measures* 15; cf. Stein, *Jesus, the Temple, and the Coming Son of Man*, 94.

The people of the church in Jerusalem had been commanded by a revelation, vouchsafed to approved men there before the war, to leave the city and to dwell in a certain town of Perea called Pella. And after the flight of those who believed in Christ, the Justice of God then visited upon them all their acts of violence to Christ and his apostles, by destroying that generation of wicked persons root and branch from among men.[12]

Before concluding his discussion of the destruction of Jerusalem and the temple, Jesus commented on the severity of the tribulation his followers would encounter. The great tribulation of the siege and destruction of Jerusalem is described as the worst in human history. If God were not to cut the days short, there wouldn't be any survivors. The language seems so extreme that many interpreters assume Jesus is here talking about a final "great tribulation" that would come at the end of human history, but there has been no indication yet that Jesus has switched from answering the disciples' question about the destruction of the temple to start talking about the end of the age. More likely, Jesus is using common hyperbolic language to describe such a disaster for which any lesser description would be inadequate.

Hyperbolic Language of Disaster

1. "Behold, about this time tomorrow I will cause very heavy hail to fall, such as never has been in Egypt from the day it was founded until now." (Exod. 9:18)

2. "There shall be a great cry throughout all the land of Egypt, *such as there has never been, nor ever will be again.*" (Exod. 11:6, emphasis added)

3. "Like blackness there is spread upon the mountains a great and powerful people; their like has never been before, nor will be again after them through the years of all generations." (Joel 2:2)

4. "So there was great distress in Israel, such as had not been since the time that prophets ceased to appear among them." (1 Macc. 9:27)

---

12. James Stevenson, *A New Eusebius: Documents Illustrating the History of the Church to AD 337* (London: SPCK, 1987), 5.

The "elect" for whom God would shorten the days were either Christians who somehow were still trapped in the city or faithful and innocent Jews who had been caught up in the carnage of the revolutionaries. Josephus reports that one million one hundred thousand died in the siege and ninety-seven thousand were taken prisoner by the Romans (*Jewish War* 6.420). Other descriptions of the siege confirm Jesus' prophetic description of the great tribulation of that time. Luke describes the great distress with more specificity: People would fall by the sword and be taken captive.

Descriptions of the Siege

1. "The roofs were thronged with women and babes completely exhausted, the alleys with the corpses of the aged; children and youths, with swollen figures, roamed like phantoms through the market-places and collapsed wherever their doom overtook them. As for burying their relatives, the sick had not the strength, while those with vigor still left were deterred both by the multitude of the dead and by the uncertainty of their own fate. For many fell dead while burying others, and many went forth to their tombs ere fate was upon them. And amidst these calamities there was neither lamentation nor wailing: famine stifled the emotions and with dry eyes and grinning mouths these slowly dying victims looked on those who had gone to their rest before them." (Josephus, *Jewish War* 5.513–15)

2. "I am here about to describe an act *unparalleled in the history* whether of Greeks or barbarians. . . . Among the residents of the region beyond the Jordan was a woman named Mary, daughter of Eleazar. . . . Seizing her child, an infant at the breast . . . she slew her son, and then, having roasted the body and devoured half of it, she covered up and stored the remainder." (Josephus, *Jewish War* 6.199, 201, 205, 208)

3. "Indeed, in my opinion, the misfortunes *of all nations since the world began* fall short of those of the Jews." (Josephus, *Jewish War* 1.12)

Luke concludes Jesus' answer about the destruction of the temple by noting that the city would be trampled by the Gentiles until the times of the Gentiles would be fulfilled. Jesus thus introduced an indefinite period ("the times of the Gentiles") into the discussion. This is important for our purposes because it marks a clear distinction between Jesus' discussion of the near future (the destruction of Jerusalem in the year 70) and the distant future (the second coming and end of the age). Everything in the Olivet Discourse in Matthew, Mark, and Luke up to this point has been Jesus' answer to the disciples' question about when the temple would be destroyed, and Luke's Gospel makes clear that after the destruction of the temple there would be an indefinite period before the next events discussed by Jesus, his coming, and the end of the age. But we are getting slightly ahead of ourselves; Matthew and Mark both contain a few more verses that are not included in Luke's Gospel.

Imposters

Matthew 24:23–28

[23] *Then* if anyone says to you, 'Look, here is the Christ!' or 'There he is!' do not believe it. [24] For false christs and false prophets will arise and perform great signs and wonders, so as to lead astray, if possible, even the elect. [25] *See, I have told you beforehand.* [26] So, if they say to you, 'Look, he is in the wilderness,' do not go out. If they say, 'Look, he is in the inner rooms,' do not believe it. [27] For as the lightning comes from the east and shines as far as the west, so will be the coming of the Son of Man. [28] Wherever the corpse is, there the vultures will gather.

Mark 13:21–23

[21] And *then* if anyone says to you, 'Look, here is the Christ!' or 'Look, there he is!' do not believe it. [22] For false christs and false prophets will arise and perform signs and wonders, to lead astray, if possible, the elect. [23] But be on guard; *I have told you all things beforehand.*

Matthew and Mark both follow up the description of tribulation with the temporal adverb "then," which could indicate events contemporaneous or subsequent to the destruction of Jerusalem. Unlike Luke, Matthew and Mark have no indication that Jesus is finished discussing the destruction of the temple, and false messiahs and false prophets certainly characterized the period of the years 66–70. On the other hand, Jesus may be transitioning in his answer to the events that would ensue after the year 70. If this is the case, he is warning his disciples that even after the temple would be destroyed, false messiahs and false prophets would be a danger to the community. The past two thousand years of history have certainly borne out the validity of this prophecy. Throughout the discourse, Jesus had stressed the importance of being on guard against deception by false messiahs and false prophets (Matt. 24:4–5, 9–13).

Matthew records two extra verses to help protect Christians from deception. When the Son of Man comes, this won't be a secret coming; it will be evident to all. Lightning and circling vultures are obvious sights that cannot be hidden in secret but are visible to everyone. In the same way, Jesus' future coming won't be hidden, secret, or easy to miss. These verses are a challenge to interpreters who argue that the coming of the Son of Man—Jesus—was his coming/going to the Father and enthronement at the Father's right hand, since that enthronement was not visible to people on earth. The verses also appear to pose a challenge to those who think that there will be a secret coming of Jesus to rapture his followers ahead of his final coming. The New Testament teaches explicitly about only one visible and public return of Jesus.

Just as Luke made clear that Jesus was ending his discussion of the destruction of Jerusalem with his mention of the indefinite period called "the times of the Gentiles," Mark indicates a transition in the topic of the Olivet Discourse with the phrase "I have told you all things beforehand." This phrase likely signals that in Mark Jesus is moving on from answering the question about the timing of the destruction of the temple to the question of his coming and the end of the age. This could apply to Matthew as well but is clearest in Mark's account since there are three connections between the beginning of the discourse and Mark 13:23.[13]

First, the disciples asked when "these things" would happen and what sign would indicate that "all these things" would be accomplished (13:4), and here Jesus states that he told them "all things" beforehand (13:23). Second, Mark begins Jesus' answer by saying "Jesus *began to say* to them"

---

13. For further discussion of these three points see Stein, *Jesus, the Temple, and the Coming Son of Man*, 100.

(13:5), while here Jesus says "I *have told* you all things *beforehand*" (13:23). Third, Jesus began the discourse with a warning to watch out or be on their guard ("beware" or *blepete* in Greek), and here he repeats the warning to "be on guard" (*blepete* again).[14]

Individually, these points may not seem significant, but together they point to a distinct section running from 13:5–23, which is directed toward answering the question of the disciples in 13:4. Beginning in 13:24, Jesus moves on to the second topic of his coming and the end of the age. Matthew is probably similar here, although the use of "then" may indicate that these verses in Matthew and Mark have a dual function and are both concluding the discussion of the destruction of the temple and describing a transitional period between that destruction and the distant future coming of the Son of Man. If so, this transitional period would correspond to Luke's "time of the Gentiles" and extend to us in the present.

Answering the Disciples' First Question

Jesus began answering the disciples' question about when the temple would be destroyed by describing several things that would happen first and that would not signal the end: false messiahs, wars, rumors of war, famines, earthquakes, persecution, betrayal, and false prophets (Mark 13:5–13 and parallels in Matthew and Luke). He then described a terrible period of tribulation associated with the desolation of the Jerusalem temple before the temple and city would be destroyed and trampled by Gentiles (Mark 13:14–23 and parallels). If the Olivet Discourse ended at this point, there would be very little debate; its meaning would be obvious. The disciples asked Jesus when the temple would be destroyed, and his answer addressed that question. In the following verses of the discourse, however, Jesus described events which, if understood literally, didn't occur when Jerusalem was destroyed by the Romans in the year 70. It is very likely that Jesus here transitions to answer the second question recorded in Matthew's Gospel: "What will be the sign of your coming and of the close of the age?" (Matt 24:3).

---

14. The ESV obscures this point by translating the same Greek word differently in Mark 13:5 and 23.

Chapter 3

Cosmic Upheaval and the
Coming of the Son of Man

In the last chapter we suggested that everything so far in the Olivet Discourse has been Jesus' answer to the disciples' question about when the temple would be destroyed (with perhaps Matt. 24:23–28 and Mark 13:21–23 functioning as both a conclusion and a transition to this section on the coming of the Son of Man).[1] Jesus didn't just listen to the disciples' question about the temple and give them an entirely unrelated answer; he answered their question with a threefold prophetic description of (1) events that wouldn't constitute the sign (false messiahs, wars, famines, earthquakes, persecutions, etc.), (2) the sign itself (the abomination of desolation), and (3) the terrible suffering and tribulation of the judgment on Jerusalem that would lead to the destruction of the temple.

Everything Jesus described so far in the Olivet Discourse was fulfilled during the years 30–70. There is nothing in the Olivet Discourse up to this point indicating that Jesus has begun to talk about a distant future event unrelated to the destruction of Jerusalem and the temple in the year 70. There is no indication that he is referring to the end-time rapture, a seven-year period of tribulation, or the destruction of a rebuilt Jerusalem. The discourse is solidly grounded in Jesus' original historical situation as a response to his disciples' question as to when the current temple would

---

1. We do recognize some possible intentional ambiguity in Matthew by which his account intertwines the two main events (i.e., the year 70 and Jesus' second coming). This is possibly the case with Matthew's reference to proclamation of the gospel to all nations before the end (24:14) and the false prophets and messiahs who would come after the destruction of the temple (24:23–24).

be destroyed. In the following section, however, there are good reasons to think that Jesus transitioned to answer the second question (included only in Matthew's Gospel) about his coming and the end of the age.

Cosmic Upheaval and the Coming of the Son of Man

Matthew 24:29–31	Mark 13:24–27	Luke 21:25–28
[29] "Immediately after the tribulation of those days the sun will be darkened, and the moon will not give its light, and the stars will fall from heaven, and the powers of the heavens will be shaken.	[24] "But in those days, after that tribulation, the sun will be darkened, and the moon will not give its light, [25] and the stars will be falling from heaven, and the powers in the heavens will be shaken.	[25] "And there will be signs in sun and moon and stars, and on the earth distress of nations in perplexity because of the roaring of the sea and the waves, [26] people fainting with fear and with foreboding of what is coming on the world. For the powers of the heavens will be shaken. [27] And then they will see the Son of Man coming in a cloud with power and great glory. [28] Now when these things begin to take place, straighten up and raise your heads, because your redemption is drawing near."
[30] Then will appear in heaven the sign of the Son of Man, and then all the tribes of the earth will mourn, and they will see the Son of Man coming on the clouds of heaven with power and great glory. [31] And he will send out his angels with a loud trumpet call, and they will gather his elect from the four winds, from one end of heaven to the other."	[26] And then they will see the Son of Man coming in clouds with great power and glory. [27] And then he will send out the angels and gather his elect from the four winds, from the ends of the earth to the ends of heaven.	

At this point in the Olivet Discourse, Jesus seems to transition from discussing the destruction of Jerusalem to his future coming and the end of the age. The clarity of Luke's account in the preceding verse (21:24) suggests this conclusion since the destruction of Jerusalem is separated from this cosmic upheaval by an indefinite period, the time of the Gentiles (the past two thousand years, and counting).

Before moving on, we need to explore the main alternative approach to interpreting these verses describing cosmic upheaval and the coming of the

Son of Man. This alternative approach is often associated in some way with preterism and is most forcefully advocated by two eminent biblical scholars, R. T. France and N. T. Wright.[2] These scholars argue that the language of cosmic upheaval and the coming of the Son of Man in the Olivet Discourse does not point to the distant future but is still focused on the events of the year 70. Even if this may seem far-fetched, the arguments of these scholars appear cogent, at least at first glance, if not persuasive. We'll present their most compelling arguments and explain why we're not convinced. Interested readers are encouraged to read their writings for themselves.

Four points are worth mentioning in support of the interpretation that Jesus' discussion of cosmic upheaval and the coming of the Son of Man was fulfilled in the events of the year 70. First, Jesus seemed to claim that the cosmic upheaval and coming of the Son of Man would take place within that generation.

Matthew 24:34	Mark 13:30	Luke 21:32
Truly, I say to you, this generation will not pass away until all these things take place.	Truly, I say to you, this generation will not pass away until all these things take place.	Truly, I say to you, this generation will not pass away until all has taken place.

A straightforward reading of these verses would seem to suggest that "all these things" are all the matters referenced in the Olivet Discourse up to this point, including the cosmic upheaval and coming of the Son of Man. All these things would take place within "this generation," so everything in the Olivet Discourse up to this point relates to the year 70.

Second, Matthew introduces the cosmic upheaval with the phrase "immediately after the tribulation of those days." This would seem to suggest rather strongly that Jesus' coming will immediately follow the great tribulation of the destruction of Jerusalem and the temple and not be separated by thousands of years.

---

2. Of course, there are other interpreters who support this view, but R. T. France and N. T. Wright are perhaps the most influential proponents. Where they differ, R. T. France's arguments are more compelling in his recognition that there is a focus on Jesus' second coming (*parousia*) in Matthew 24:36–25:46 and Mark 13:32–37. See France, *Gospel of Matthew*; France, *Gospel of Mark*; Wright, *Jesus and the Victory of God*.

Third, the language of cosmic upheaval is drawn from the Old Testament prophets who regularly used such language in a hyperbolic way to describe the destruction of major cities by human armies. The prophets describe the sun and moon being darkened and the stars falling to describe earthshaking events that didn't involve literal cosmic upheaval.

Fourth, the language of "the Son of Man coming on the clouds of heaven" is drawn from Daniel 7:13, which describes the Son of Man going to the Father to receive his kingdom. It is suggested that this is a reference to the enthronement of Jesus at God's right hand in heaven and not to his second coming to earth.

This interpretation is possible and makes good sense of Matthew's use of "immediately after the tribulation of those days" and the comment in Matthew, Mark, and Luke that "all these things" will take place in "this generation." That said, the fact that an interpretation is *possible* does not necessarily make it *probable*. We'll first respond to the four points noted above before explaining why we think this interpretation of cosmic upheaval and the coming of the Son of Man is improbable.

First, this interpretation rightly stresses the fact that "this generation" indicates the current generation alive at the time. Jesus did indeed claim that the destruction of the temple would take place within a generation. He provided a specific timetable that was proved correct by the unfolding events of history. But does this require that "all these things" indicates everything in the Olivet Discourse up to that point? The language of "all these things" is drawn from the initial question concerning when the temple would be destroyed.

Matthew 24:3	Mark 13:3–4	Luke 21:7
[3] As he sat on the Mount of Olives, the disciples came to him privately, saying, "Tell us, when will *these things* be, and what will be the sign of your coming and of the end of the age?"	[3] And as he sat on the Mount of Olives opposite the temple, Peter and James and John and Andrew asked him privately, [4] "Tell us, when will *these things* be, and what will be the sign when *all these things* are about to be accomplished?"	[7] And they asked him, "Teacher, when will these things be, and what will be the sign when *these things* are about to take place?"

Matt 24:34	Mark 13:30	Luke 21:32
[34] Truly, I say to you, this generation will not pass away until *all these things* take place. [35] Heaven and earth will pass away, but my words will not pass away.	[30] Truly, I say to you, this generation will not pass away until *all these things* take place. [31] Heaven and earth will pass away, but my words will not pass away.	[32] Truly, I say to you, this generation will not pass away until *all* has taken place. [33] Heaven and earth will pass away, but my words will not pass away.
[36] "*But* concerning *that* day and hour no one knows, not even the angels of heaven, nor the Son, but the Father only.	[32] "*But* concerning *that* day or that hour, no one knows, not even the angels in heaven, nor the Son, but only the Father.	(Absent from Luke)

Now "these things" and "all these things" aren't technical phrases and don't always point to the same events, but their use here should be connected back to the disciples' question about the temple. This would mean that all the things mentioned about the destruction of the temple would take place within that generation but not necessarily everything Jesus spoke about up to that point in the Olivet Discourse.

The idea that "all these things" indicates the comments about the destruction of the temple and not everything Jesus said in the Olivet Discourse up to that point is strengthened by looking at the verses that follow Jesus' statement about "this generation" in Matthew and Mark. Jesus establishes a contrast between what he does know (the destruction of the temple within a generation) and what he does not know ("that day or that hour").

This is not a contrast between a broad forty-year period and a specific day as if Jesus could predict the decade but not the day; it is a contrast between two different events. The use of the demonstrative pronoun "that" indicates that Jesus is referring to a day already mentioned in the Olivet Discourse but the contrastive conjunction "but" indicates that this day is different from all the things that will be fulfilled with the destruction of Jerusalem (Matt. 24:36; Mark 13:32).

In Matthew's account, "that day" connects back to the second part of the disciples' question concerning the coming of the Son of Man and the end of the age (Matt. 24:3) and likely points to the description of cosmic upheaval and the coming of the Son of Man described in Matthew 24:29–31, Mark 13:24–27, and Luke 21:25–28.[3]

Second, there are several possible ways to understand Jesus' comment that the cosmic upheaval and coming of the Son of Man will happen "immediately after the tribulation of those days" (Matt. 24:29). Mark more generally notes that it will happen after the tribulation of the destruction of Jerusalem without saying whether it will be immediate or distant. D. A. Carson explains the immediacy of Matthew's account by arguing that the Olivet Discourse up to this point has focused on the general period of distress and tribulation between Jesus' first and second coming, with the events of the year 70 constituting a "particularly violent display of judgment."[4]

We noted above that the non-signs (false messiahs, wars, earthquakes, famines, persecutions, etc.) were both fulfilled by the year 70 and have also characterized the whole course of human history and that the description of false messiahs and false prophets in Matthew 24:23–28 could describe the events of the year 70 and the time since then. The common early Christian perspective was that the entire period between Jesus' first and second coming was a period of tribulation, and Matthew's immediacy could be pointing to the end of this broader period of tribulation.[5] Similar to this solution, many think that "Jesus prophetically blends the tribulation of 66–70 with the final one . . . [for] the prophetic perspective naturally viewed nearer historical events as precursors of the final events."[6]

---

3. The New Testament regularly connects the future Day of the Lord with the second coming of Jesus: 1 Thessalonians 5:2; 2 Thessalonians 1:10; 2:2; 2 Peter 3:10; 1 Corinthians 5:5; Philippian 1:6, 10; 2:16. Regarding Mark 13:24–25, George R. Beasley-Murray points out that "this passage is a conflation of Old Testament allusions to the Day of the Lord" (Isa. 13:10; 34:4; Joel 2:10; 3:15–16; *Jesus and the Kingdom of God* [Grand Rapids: Eerdmans, 1986], 331).

4. D. A. Carson, "Matthew," in *The Expositor's Bible Commentary*, rev. ed., ed. Tremper Longman III and David E. Garland, vol. 9: *Matthew and Mark* (Grand Rapids: Zondervan, 2010), 557.

5. Tribulation as the present reality for Christians between Jesus' first and second coming: Matthew 13:21; Mark 4:17; John 16:33; Acts 11:19; 14:22; 20:23; Romans 5:3; 8:35; 12:12; 2 Corinthians 1:4, 8; 2:4; 4:17; 6:4; 8:2; Colossians 1:24; 1 Thessalonians 1:6; 1 Thessalonians 3:3; 2 Thessalonians 1:4; Hebrews 10:33; Revelation 1:9; 2:9, 10.

6. See Craig S. Keener, *A Commentary on the Gospel of Matthew* (Grand Rapids: Eerdmans, 1999), 577–78, who discusses this and other solutions in greater detail.

The great tribulation of the year 70 is part of the broader tribulation that will characterize the time until Jesus returns.

Third, it is true that the Old Testament prophets generally used language of cosmic upheaval to describe God's judgment of cities and nations that was executed through the more mundane means of human armies and warfare.[7] The language of cosmic upheaval in the Old Testament is linked to the language of theophany (the appearance of God) and stresses the theological truth that God himself is active in the judgment of these cities. If Jesus were using the language of cosmic upheaval in continuity with the Hebrew prophets, it would very naturally apply to the destruction of Jerusalem. It is also evident, however, that many first-century Jews and Christians understood that physical and literal cosmic upheaval would characterize the final day of judgment, and it is not at all evident that such language should be understood figuratively when applied to Jesus' second coming.[8]

Fourth, it is true that the "coming of the Son of Man" (drawing on Dan. 7:13) is sometimes applied to Jesus' enthronement at God's right hand and not to his future coming; this is particularly evident when Daniel 7:13 is combined with Psalm 110:1.[9] This does not mean, however, that every mention of the coming of the Son of Man should be understood in this way. In fact, it is much more common in the New Testament to connect the coming of the Son of Man to his future return to earth to fully establish his kingdom on earth.[10] There are several problems with interpreting the "coming of the Son of Man" in the Olivet Discourse as Jesus' enthronement at God's right hand. First, Jesus' enthronement at God's right hand took place with his ascension and not with the destruction of Jerusalem in the year 70.[11] Second, in the Olivet Discourse it is evident that people will

---

7. See Appendix 1.

8. 2 Peter 3:10; Revelation 6:12–14; 20:11.

9. Matthew 10:23; 16:28; 26:64; Mark 14:62.

10. Matthew 13:40–41; 16:27; 25:31; Mark 8:38; Acts 1:11; 1 Corinthians 11:26; 15:23, 52; 1 Thessalonians 4:15; 2 Thessalonians 2:1; Titus 2:13; 2 Peter 3:4; Revelation 1:7; *Didache* 16:7–8.

11. France unconvincingly explains this by saying "the time of the temple's destruction will also be the time when it will become clear that the Son of Man, rejected by the leaders of his people, has been vindicated and enthroned at the right hand of God, and that it is he who is now to exercise the universal kingship which is his destiny" (*Gospel of Matthew*, 924).

"see" Jesus coming.[12] It will be visible and evident to all, not an invisible enthronement at God's right hand or an invisible coming in judgment.

These responses by themselves aren't sufficient to disprove the interpretation offered by N. T. Wright and R. T. France, but there is an apparently insurmountable problem with connecting the cosmic upheaval and coming of the Son of Man with the destruction of Jerusalem in the year 70: the earliest Christians didn't seem to interpret Jesus' words in this way. We already noted how in Luke's account, Jesus distinguished the destruction of Jerusalem from the coming of the Son of Man by an indefinite period called the "time of the Gentiles." They are not the same event. We can add to this the words of the apostle Paul about Jesus' second coming. Paul wrote 1 Thessalonians before the Gospels of Matthew, Mark, and Luke were written, so his comments reflect Jesus' teaching in the Olivet Discourse before that teaching was written down in the Gospels:

> For this we declare to you *by a word from the Lord*, that we who are alive, who are left until the *coming of the Lord*, will not precede those who have fallen asleep. For the Lord himself will descend from heaven with a cry of command, with the voice of an archangel, and with the sound of *the trumpet of God*. And the dead in Christ will rise first. Then we who are alive, who are left, will be caught up together with them in the clouds to meet the Lord in the air, and so we will always be with the Lord. (1 Thess. 4:15–17)

Paul is here drawing his teaching about the future from the teaching of Jesus ("We declare to you by a word from the Lord"). He associates the second coming of Jesus with the sound of the trumpet of God and the gathering of God's people, both living and resurrected.[13] This is very similar to the way in which Jesus associated his coming in the Olivet Discourse with a loud trumpet call and the gathering of the elect from one end of heaven to another (Matt. 24:31). Following the lead of Luke and Paul, it is best to read the description of cosmic upheaval and the coming of the

---

12. See, however, the spiritual "seeing" of Matthew 26:64 and Mark 14:62 with reference to Jesus' enthronement at God's right hand.

13. Paul also connects a trumpet with the future resurrection in 1 Corinthians 15:52.

Son of Man in the Olivet Discourse as pointing forward to Jesus' second coming at the end of the age to bring judgment on God's adversaries and salvation to God's people.

The language of cosmic upheaval also shares several connections with the book of Revelation. In Revelation, we're confronted with a visionary narrative of de-creation in judgment leading forward to a re-creation, the new heavens and the new earth. The celestial bodies were commonly worshiped as deities in the ancient world, so such an upheaval would communicate that they have no power over the coming of the Son of Man. Most importantly, as noted above and in Appendix 1, such language is most commonly used in the Old Testament to describe God's coming and personal involvement in judgment.

Matthew alone mentions the sign of the Son of Man in heaven, the meaning of which has proved elusive to interpreters. The *Didache*, an ancient Christian document from the beginning of the second century, interpreted it as follows: "And then there will appear the signs of the truth: first the sign of an opening in heaven, then the sign of the sound of a trumpet, and third, the resurrection of the dead."[14] This connection of the sign to the cosmic upheaval is probably on the right track; in Matthew, the sign is closely connected with the actual coming of the Son of Man, and there is only a brief interval for mourning between the sign and the coming.

Matthew and Mark both describe the supernatural ingathering of God's people, which Luke describes as the redemption of God's people. Luke's reference to redemption doesn't point to the forgiveness of sin, which takes place at a person's conversion, but to the full restoration of all things. The ingathering of God's people echoes one of Jesus' parables with a twist:

> [40] Just as the weeds are gathered and burned with fire, so will it be at the end of the age. [41] The Son of Man will send his angels, and they will gather out of his kingdom all causes of sin and all law-breakers, [42] and throw them into the fiery furnace. In that

---

14. *Didache* 16:6. All translations from the *Didache* are from Michael W. Holmes, *The Apostolic Fathers: Greek Texts and English Translations*, 3rd ed. (Grand Rapids: Baker Academic, 2007).

place there will be weeping and gnashing of teeth. ⁴³ Then the righteous will shine like the sun in the kingdom of their Father. He who has ears, let him hear. (Matt. 13:40–43)

In the parable, the angels are sent to gather all causes of sin and all lawbreakers, while in the Olivet Discourse the angels are sent to gather God's people to Jesus at his coming. Jesus' coming will be the occasion for both final salvation and final judgment.

Truth Touches Life: All Will See

The author of the book of Hebrews explores the tension we experience every day. We know that Jesus is enthroned at God's right hand and is presently the King of kings and Lord of lords. He is the world's rightful ruler but "at present, we don't yet see everything in subjection to him" (Heb. 2:8).

We don't see his rule established over all the kingdoms on the earth. Instead, we see nations fighting nations, oppression, and horror every day in the news. Our culture is replete with signs of people's rebellion against God regarding gender roles and identities, divorce, abortion, and many other evils.

But it won't be this way forever; we know that Jesus will return and with the earliest Christians we long for that future day: "Come, Lord Jesus!" (Rev. 22:20). On that future day, our faith will become sight, every eye will see Jesus, and his kingdom will be concretely and visibly established forever.

Looking Back and Looking Forward

The first long section of the Olivet Discourse contains Jesus' answer to the disciples' question about when the temple would be destroyed (Mark 13:5–23 and parallels). With Mark 13:24–27 and parallels, Jesus transitions to his distant return to earth to establish his kingdom, judge unbelievers, and bring final salvation. This event will be accompanied by a degree of cosmic upheaval, although the hyperbolic and figurative nature of such language in the Hebrew prophets makes it impossible to know the literal extent of such language (see Appendix 1).

In the following chapter, we'll discuss how Jesus concludes the Olivet Discourse by returning to each of the main topics of Jesus' teaching regarding the future: the soon-to-be-accomplished destruction of Jerusalem in the year 70 and his distant return as the reigning Son of Man. Jesus returns to each of these topics to make specific statements about the timing of these events. This was, after all, the main query posed by the disciples. Jesus does not leave them hanging but provides specific answers to their legitimate questions.

Chapter 4

Concluding the Olivet Discourse

Up to this point in the Olivet Discourse, Jesus has discussed two distinct events: the destruction of the temple and Jerusalem in the year 70 (Mark 13:1–23 and parallels) and the coming of the Son of Man at some point after the destruction of the temple and "the times of the Gentiles" (Mark 13:24–27 and parallels; Luke 21:24). The concluding sections of the Olivet Discourse return to each of these topics to provide further information about the specific timing of the event in question and to use parables to guide Jesus' followers as they think about the future. Jesus made clear that the destruction of the temple would take place within a generation but that he didn't know the timing of his coming and the end of the age.

The Timing of the Destruction of the Temple: This Generation

Matthew 24:32–35	Mark 13:28–31	Luke 21:29–33
32 "From the fig tree learn its lesson: as soon as its branch becomes tender and puts out its leaves, you know that summer is near. 33 So also, *when you see all these things*, you know that he [it] is near, at the very gates.	28 "From the fig tree learn its lesson: as soon as its branch becomes tender and puts out its leaves, you know that summer is near. 29 So also, *when you see these things* taking place, you know that he [it] is near, at the very gates.	29 And he told them a parable: "Look at the fig tree, and all the trees. 30 As soon as they come out in leaf, you see for yourselves and know that the summer is already near. 31 So also, *when you see these things* taking place, you know that the kingdom of God is near.

Matthew 24:32–35	Mark 13:28–31	Luke 21:29–33
[34] Truly, I say to you, this generation will not pass away until *all these things* take place. [35] Heaven and earth will pass away, but my words will not pass away."	[30] Truly, I say to you, this generation will not pass away until *all these things* take place. [31] Heaven and earth will pass away, but my words will not pass away."	[32] Truly, I say to you, this generation will not pass away until all has taken place. [33] Heaven and earth will pass away, but my words will not pass away."

There are several reasons to think that with the parable of the fig tree Jesus is briefly transitioning back to conclude his answer to the disciples' question about when the temple will be destroyed and not talking about the second coming. First, we noted above that the language of "these things" and "all these things" intentionally mirrors the question of the disciples at the beginning of the Olivet Discourse. This is an indication that Jesus is concluding his answer to that question and not necessarily pointing to everything said in the Olivet Discourse up to that point (i.e., the "these things" and "all these things" do not include the second coming). Second, the parable of the fig tree is used as an illustration of how signs indicate the approach of a given event. In the case of the fig tree, the sprouting of leaves indicates the approach of summer.[1] By analogy, Jesus explained that when his followers would see certain things, they would know that a given event was near. The language mirrors the language used earlier in the Olivet Discourse concerning the abomination of desolation, which would be a sign indicating the destruction of Jerusalem.

Matthew 24:15	Mark 13:14	Luke 21:20
[15] "So *when you see* the abomination of *desolation* spoken of by the prophet Daniel, standing in the holy place (let the reader understand).	[14] "But *when you see* the abomination of *desolation* standing where he ought not to be (let the reader understand), then let those who are in Judea flee to the mountains.	[20] "But *when you see* Jerusalem surrounded by armies, then know that its *desolation* has come near.

---

1. Luke's addition of the phrase "and all the trees" indicates that there is no deeper or symbolic meaning to the fig tree; it is not allegorically referring to the rebirth of the nation of Israel. Any deciduous tree would work for the illustration; it just happened that fig trees were common in Palestine and there could have very well been a fig tree sprouting leaves nearby (Passover took place in the spring).

Matthew 24:33	Mark 13:29	Luke 21:31
[33] So also, *when you see all these things*, you know that he [it] is near, at the very gates."	[29] So also, *when you see these things* taking place, you know that he [it] is near, at the very gates."	[31] So also, *when you see these things* taking place, you know that the kingdom of God is near."

These two verbal connections—"these things" and "when you see"—are strong indications that Jesus is here concluding his answer to the question about when the temple would be destroyed. This conclusion helps with a translation difficulty. The Greek text in Matthew and Mark only uses a third person singular verb, so the context must determine whether he, she, or it is near. If the translator thinks Jesus is using the fig tree parable to describe his second coming, the context would suggest "he" (as in the ESV throughout), but if the translator thinks Jesus is referring to the destruction of Jerusalem, "it" would be a better translation (as suggested by us in brackets in the chart above). When the disciples were going to witness the events Jesus had predicted, particularly the ritual desecration of the temple—the abomination of desolation—and the approach of Roman armies, they would know that "it [the destruction of the city] was near."

This conclusion is confirmed by Jesus' plain answer to the question about the timing of the temple's destruction: It would take place within that generation. The various attempts to explain "this generation" as a general way to describe the present age, the race of the Jews, or the final generation living when Jesus returns are rendered unlikely by the way in which Jesus regularly used the phrase "this generation" throughout the Gospels to describe the generation of people alive at the time.

This Generation

1. "But to what shall I compare *this generation*? It is like children sitting in the marketplaces and calling to their playmates." (Matt. 11:16)

2. "But he answered them, 'An evil and adulterous *generation* seeks for a sign, but no sign will be given to it except the sign of the prophet Jonah.' . . . The men of Nineveh will rise up at the judgment with *this generation* and condemn it, for they repented at the preaching

of Jonah, and behold, something greater than Jonah is here. The queen of the South will rise up at the judgment with *this generation* and condemn it, for she came from the ends of the earth to hear the wisdom of Solomon, and behold, something greater than Solomon is here. . . .Then it goes and brings with it seven other spirits more evil than itself, and they enter and dwell there, and the last state of that person is worse than the first. So also will it be with *this evil generation.*" (Matt. 12:39, 41–42, 45)

3. "An *evil and adulterous generation* seeks for a sign, but no sign will be given to it except the sign of Jonah." (Matt. 16:4)

4. "And Jesus answered, 'O faithless and twisted *generation*, how long am I to be with you? How long am I to bear with you?' (Matt. 17:17)

5. "Truly, I say to you, all these things will come upon *this generation.*" (Matt. 23:36)

6. "And he sighed deeply in his spirit and said, 'Why does *this generation* seek a sign? Truly, I say to you, no sign will be given to *this generation.*'" (Mark 8:12)

7. "For whoever is ashamed of me and of my words in this adulterous and sinful *generation*, of him will the Son of Man also be ashamed when he comes in the glory of his Father with the holy angels." (Mark 8:38)

8. "And he answered them, 'O faithless *generation*, how long am I to be with you? How long am I to bear with you?'" (Mark 9:19)

9. "To what then shall I compare the people of *this generation*, and what are they like?" (Luke 7:31)

10. "Jesus answered, 'O faithless and twisted *generation*, how long am I to be with you and bear with you?'" (Luke 9:41)

11. "When the crowds were increasing, he began to say, '*This generation* is an evil *generation*. It seeks for a sign, but no sign will be given to it except the sign of Jonah. For as Jonah became a sign to the people of Nineveh, so will the Son of Man be to *this generation*. The

queen of the South will rise up at the judgment with the men of *this generation* and condemn them, for she came from the ends of the earth to hear the wisdom of Solomon, and behold, something greater than Solomon is here. The men of Nineveh will rise up at the judgment with *this generation* and condemn it, for they repented at the preaching of Jonah, and behold, something greater than Jonah is here.'" (Luke 11:29–32)

12. "Therefore also the Wisdom of God said, 'I will send them prophets and apostles, some of whom they will kill and persecute,' so that the blood of all the prophets, shed from the foundation of the world, may be charged against *this generation*, from the blood of Abel to the blood of Zechariah, who perished between the altar and the sanctuary. Yes, I tell you, it will be required of *this generation*." (Luke 11:49–51)

13. "But first he must suffer many things and be rejected by *this generation*." (Luke 17:25)

Jesus frequently spoke about this current generation, generally with a focus on judgment; this is exactly what we find in the Olivet Discourse.

Instead of "it is near, at the very gates," Luke notes that "the kingdom of God is near." It is commonly recognized that Jesus spoke about the kingdom of God in an already/not yet manner. Sometimes Jesus focused on the fact that the kingdom of God was already a present reality because of his own life and ministry.[2] With Jesus' life, death, resurrection, and enthronement at God's right hand, the kingdom of God has been established and is already here. The kingdom of God has been inaugurated but not yet been consummated. It is a present reality but not yet seen and recognized by all; in fact, it is actively opposed by many. Jesus also taught about the future consummation of the kingdom and associated it with his second coming.[3] Our previous discussion of "these things," "when you see," and "this generation" indicates that the kingdom of God is associated in Luke with the destruction of Jerusalem, referring to the kingdom

---

2. Matthew 3:2; 10:7; Mark 1:15; Luke 10:9, 11; 11:20; 17:21.
3. Luke 11:2; 14:15; 17:20.

that has already been inaugurated and is currently growing and expanding throughout the world. The destruction of the temple could be linked to the proclamation and growth of the kingdom by making clear that forgiveness of sins couldn't be obtained by temple sacrifices but only in Jesus and that God's people could no longer be ethnically limited to the people of Israel but now included all the nations on the earth.

An astounding point emerges when we compare the closing verse of this section with Matthew 5:18, which reads, "For truly, I say to you, until heaven and earth pass away, not an iota, not a dot, will pass from the Law until all is accomplished." Jesus had earlier emphasized the permanence of God's word revealed in the Old Testament law; here in the Olivet Discourse he describes his *own* words with an even *greater* level of permanence: His words will never pass away! He is staking an astounding claim to authority beyond the divine revelation of the Old Testament. Jesus' words are more certain and reliable than creation itself.

The Timing of Jesus' Return

Matthew 24:36	Mark 13:32–37	Luke 21:34–36
36 But concerning that day and hour no one knows, not even the angels of heaven, nor the Son, but the Father only.	32 But concerning that day or that hour, no one knows, not even the angels in heaven, nor the Son, but only the Father.	
	33 Be on guard, keep awake. For you do not know when the time will come. 34 It is like a man going on a journey, when he leaves home and puts his servants in charge, each with his work, and commands the doorkeeper to stay awake.	34 But watch yourselves lest your hearts be weighed down with dissipation and drunkenness and cares of this life, and that day come upon you suddenly like a trap. 35 For it will come upon all who dwell on the face of the whole earth.

Mark 13:32–37	Luke 21:34–36
[35] Therefore stay awake—for you do not know when the master of the house will come, in the evening, or at midnight, or when the rooster crows, or in the morning— [36] lest he come suddenly and find you asleep. [37] And what I say to you I say to all: Stay awake.	[36] But stay awake at all times, praying that you may have strength to escape all these things that are going to take place, and to stand before the Son of Man.

Matthew and Mark both begin with a clear indication of a shift in topic from the destruction of Jerusalem to Jesus' second coming: "But concerning." Jesus prophetically indicated that Jerusalem would be destroyed in judgment within a generation but indicated that he didn't know the timing of *that* day or hour. As discussed above, "that" day should be linked with the coming of the Son of Man, that is, Jesus' return.[4] Luke may have omitted the verse because it could have been seen by some as an embarrassment; Jesus was claiming not to know the timing of something as important as the future consummation. The verse indicates both a distinction between Jesus and the Father and between Jesus and the angels. As the author of Hebrews affirms, Jesus is far superior to the angels while his identity cannot simply be collapsed into that of God the Father.

This verse and the following parables provide a strong contrast between the destruction of Jerusalem in the year 70 and the second coming of Jesus. The destruction of Jerusalem would be preceded by warning signs that could be heeded to avoid the danger and would take place within a generation. In contrast, the second coming would be sudden, take the world by surprise, and occur at a distant, unknown time.

This concluding section of the Olivet Discourse focuses on watchfulness—Jesus' followers must remain alert and active in obedience to his

---

4. The New Testament regularly connects the future Day of the Lord with the second coming of Jesus: 1 Thessalonians 5:2; 2 Thessalonians 1:10; 2:2; 2 Peter 3:10; 1 Corinthians 5:5; Philippians 1:6, 10; 2:16.

commands. This constant vigilance is necessary because no one knows the end; no one knows or can predict when Jesus will return. Mark emphasizes this point with a parable of a man going on a journey.[5] The workers must stay awake because they have no idea when the master will return. Jesus expands the application of this parable beyond the initial disciples when he states, "What I say to you I say to all: Stay awake" (Mark 13:37). The message of the parable applies to any and every hearer of Jesus' words: We must remain vigilant and alert.

Truth Touches Life: Stay Awake!

How do we "stay awake"? What puts us to sleep? The reference to drunkenness points to addictions that dull our senses while the reference to the cares of this life points to all the various things that could consume our mind with worry.

There is a special danger for our current generation in the explosion of technology: addiction to entertainment. With mobile devices, more and more people are becoming addicted to various forms of entertainment: sports, games, TV shows, and movies. We fear that many Christians are entertaining themselves into states of spiritual lethargy. Entertainment is not bad in and of itself, but we need to guard against every form of addiction.

Entertainment is subtle because it is not as obviously sinful as drugs or sexual addiction, but any addiction will enslave us and hinder our effectiveness in God's kingdom. Are we spending too much time being entertained? Are we addicted to entertainment?

The parable is punctuated with exhortations: "Be on guard, keep awake . . . stay awake . . . stay awake." Luke's account lacks the parable but

---

5. This parable shares similarities with other parables (Matt. 24:43–44, 45–51; 25:14–30; Luke 12:35–38, 39–40, 42–46; 19:12–27). This indicates that the broad themes were common in Jesus' teaching across various settings.

shares similar exhortations: "Watch yourselves . . . stay awake at all times, praying." Luke describes the danger of not staying awake—our hearts will become weighed down with overindulgence, drunkenness, and the cares of this life. This is a real danger confronting every one of us. That future day will not just affect Israel but the whole earth and come unexpectedly, like a trap.

The imagery of a trap implies suddenness and unexpectedness. The warning against drunkenness applies literally but also likely has a metaphorical application—many addictions are like alcoholism, which can derail a person's life and render them ineffective. Jesus is quite clear that our actions matter. How we live matters, and we'll have to give an account for our actions on that final day.

Luke stresses this point when he notes that all will stand before the Son of Man. Mark and Luke thus end the Olivet Discourse with warnings and exhortations to stay alert, active, and vigilant in anticipation of Jesus' second coming. This gets right at the issue of our response. How are we responding to the reality that Jesus will come again and we'll all have to give an account for our actions? Are we ready for Jesus' return?

Matthew's Ending

Matthew 24:37–51	Luke 17:26–36
[37] For as were the days of Noah, so will be the coming of the Son of Man. [38] For as in those days before the flood they were eating and drinking, marrying and giving in marriage, until the day when Noah entered the ark, [39] and they were unaware until the flood came and swept them all away, so will be the coming of the Son of Man. [40] Then two men will be in the field; one will be taken and one left. [41] Two women will be grinding at the mill; one will be taken and one left. [42] Therefore, stay awake, for you do not know on what day your Lord is coming.	[26] Just as it was in the days of Noah, so will it be in the days of the Son of Man. [27] They were eating and drinking and marrying and being given in marriage, until the day when Noah entered the ark, and the flood came and destroyed them all. [28] Likewise, just as it was in the days of Lot—they were eating and drinking, buying and selling, planting and building, [29] but on the day when Lot went out from Sodom, fire and sulfur rained from heaven and destroyed them all— [30] so will it be on the day when the Son of Man is revealed. [31] On that day, let the one who is on the housetop, with his goods in the house, not come

Matthew 24:37–51

Luke 17:26–36

down to take them away, and likewise let the one who is in the field not turn back. [32] Remember Lot's wife. [33] Whoever seeks to preserve his life will lose it, but whoever loses his life will keep it. [34] I tell you, in that night there will be two in one bed. One will be taken and the other left. [35] There will be two women grinding together. One will be taken and the other left."

Luke 12:39–40

[43] But know this, that if the master of the house had known in what part of the night the thief was coming, he would have stayed awake and would not have let his house be broken into. [44] Therefore you also must be ready, for the Son of Man is coming at an hour you do not expect.

[45] "Who then is the faithful and wise servant, whom his master has set over his household, to give them their food at the proper time? [46] Blessed is that servant whom his master will find so doing when he comes. [47] Truly, I say to you, he will set him over all his possessions. [48] But if that wicked servant says to himself, 'My master is delayed,'[49] and begins to beat his fellow servants and eats and drinks with drunkards, [50] the master of that servant will come on a day when he does not expect him and at an hour he does not know [51] and will cut him in pieces and put him with the hypocrites. In that place there will be weeping and gnashing of teeth.

[39] But know this, that if the master of the house had known at what hour the thief was coming, he would not have left his house to be broken into. [40] You also must be ready, for the Son of Man is coming at an hour you do not expect."

Mark and Luke conclude their versions of the Olivet Discourse with the prior section, but Matthew includes quite a bit more material, particularly if the parables of Matthew 25 are included. Luke has very similar material but places it in different locations in his Gospel. This is a likely indication that the Olivet Discourse does officially end where Mark and Luke indicate; but Jesus also taught about his second coming on different occasions, and Matthew and Luke placed this additional teaching about the second coming in what they deemed to be appropriate places in their respective Gospels. We noted at the beginning of this chapter that at many points the Gospels are arranged topically rather than chronologically; this is a good example of that phenomenon.

Matthew adds this teaching material from Jesus to the end of the Olivet Discourse because it thematically fits the theme of Jesus' second coming. This extended ending shares many themes with Mark's ending, including the suddenness of Jesus' return and the need for Jesus' followers to stay alert. Matthew adds a unique comparison with the judgment that came upon Noah's generation that Luke also included earlier in his Gospel. People in Noah's day were going about life as usual. They ate, drank, married, and went about life without preparing for the flood that came suddenly and took them all away in judgment. In this example, you would want to be one of the ones left behind because the ones swept away were taken away in judgment or, as Luke describes it, destroyed. Luke uniquely adds a comparison with the days of Lot in which people were also going about their lives as normal when judgment came suddenly and irreversibly.

These verses are often used to support the idea that Jesus will come to take away his people before the judgment comes, but the point in both Matthew and Luke is that when the Son of Man comes, it is God's people who will be left while all others will be taken away in judgment.[6] There is no hint of rapture in theses verses. The blessedness of being left behind is confirmed by the summary of the flood in Genesis 7:23: "He blotted out every living thing that was on the face of the ground, man and animals and creeping things and birds of the heavens. They were blotted out from the earth. Only Noah *was left*, and those who were with him in the

---

6. For further discussion see Benjamin L. Merkle, "Who Will Be Left Behind? Rethinking the Meaning of Matthew 24:40–41 and Luke 17:34–35," *WTJ* (2010): 169–79.

ark." You and I want to be left behind since the ones taken are taken in judgment.

Matthew 24 concludes with two parables that stress the need for believers to stay alert and prepared for Jesus' return which would come unexpectedly, like a thief. Faithful and alert believers have nothing to fear, but in the parable judgment is reserved for those who abandon their work, abuse and harm others, and lose themselves in addictions. With the closing of Matthew 24 we come to the end of Jesus' famous Olivet Discourse.

Conclusion of Part 1

We've reached the end of the Olivet Discourse and can succinctly summarize our position about which sections relate to the events of the year 70 and which relate to the second coming. We have argued that Mark 13:5–23 (and parallels in Matthew and Luke) relate to the destruction of the temple, 13:24–27 refers to the future second coming of Jesus as traditionally understood, 13:28–31 provides a parable about the destruction of the temple and concludes that topic, and 13:32–37 provides a parable about the second coming and concludes that topic. This understanding of the Olivet Discourse seems to be the best interpretation of all the available evidence.[7]

In the Olivet Discourse, Jesus thus focuses on two future events. One of these events, the destruction of the temple, was in Jesus' near future (his current generation) and is in our past. The other event, Jesus' return, has not yet taken place and is still future. Every generation of Christians must remain vigilant and be active in the Father's work because that day will come unexpectedly, and when it comes, there will be no time to prepare.

Several conclusions arise from the reading of the Olivet Discourse argued for above. First, readers who view the Olivet Discourse as referring exclusively to events associated with a seven-year period of tribulation between the rapture and Jesus' second coming may want to reconsider their view of Jesus' reference to "this generation" and the way in which the Olivet Discourse is a specific answer to a question from the disciples about when the temple would be destroyed. Jesus didn't ignore their question or give them an entirely unrelated answer. Nothing in the Olivet Discourse indicates that Jesus taught a future rapture of believers that would be followed by a seven-year period of tribulation centered on the Jewish people and Jerusalem. Jesus' comments about the tribulation and destruction of Jerusalem and the temple relate to the terrible judgment of the year 70. This, of course, doesn't mean that there won't be a rapture, an end-time

---

7. This approach is not novel or unique, and more detailed arguments for this conclusion can be found in the following sources: William L. Lane, *The Gospel According to Mark*, NICNT (Grand Rapids: Eerdmans, 1974), 455–84; Larry W. Hurtado, *Mark*, NIBC (Peabody, MA: Hendrickson, 1983), 222–25; Ben Witherington III, *The Gospel of Mark: A Socio-Rhetorical Commentary* (Grand Rapids: Eerdmans, 2001), 348–50; Stein, *Jesus, the Temple, and the Coming Son of Man*, 122.

tribulation, or a second coming—just that this portion of Scripture does not pertain to these end-time events.

Second, conversely, readers who seek to interpret all of the Olivet Discourse as referring to the destruction of the temple in the year 70 unduly minimize the importance of Matthew's expanded question at the beginning of the discourse and the way in which Jesus' words in the discourse about cosmic upheaval and the coming of the Son of Man were understood by the earliest Christians (or at least by Paul and Matthew).

We have argued that Jesus answered both questions at the beginning of Matthew's Gospel concerning when the temple would be destroyed and when Jesus would come and the current age would come to an end. Luke guides us in knowing when Jesus transitioned from speaking about the destruction of the temple to his future coming. An indefinite period, called "the times of the Gentiles," separates the two events (Luke 21:24). This is the period in which we continue to live as we wait for Jesus' return to establish his kingdom fully and finally on earth.

Part 1 has focused almost exclusively on the Olivet Discourse because it is the longest block of teaching material related to the future in the Gospels, but each Gospel also contains other material related to the future. In Part 2 we will explore each of the four main topics that Jesus addressed regarding the future. Each of these has already been hinted at or developed in the Olivet Discourse but there are many other passages throughout the Gospels in which Jesus provided further insight into these topics.

Other Teachings of Jesus about the Future in the Gospels

Introduction to Part 2

In Part 1 we explored how Jesus prophesied about two distinct events in the Olivet Discourse: the destruction of Jerusalem in the year 70 and his second coming at some point after that time. Jesus also predicted future persecution, and there are indications in the Olivet Discourse that the coming of the Son of Man will involve judgment and salvation. In Part 2 we will consider all of Jesus' teaching about the future in the Synoptic Gospels (Matthew, Mark, and Luke) outside the Olivet Discourse. When Jesus spoke about the future, he tended to focus on four broad themes pertaining to the near and more distant future that we saw in the Olivet Discourse.

Regarding the near future, Jesus prophesied that there would be (1) persecution of his followers and (2) a judgment of "this generation" with particular focus on the Jewish religious leadership for their rejection of him. Regarding the more distant future, Jesus taught that (3) the Son of Man would come with power and (4) there would be a future resurrection, final judgment, eternal reward and punishment. The first two themes are important to include because they highlight the fact that not everything Jesus predicted about the future concerns the distant future; he often prophesied concerning his immediate followers and the current generation alive at the time.

The following chapters will explore these four themes in Matthew, Mark, and Luke outside of the Olivet Discourse (but with reference to it when helpful) and will highlight any unique or distinctive teachings preserved in each individual Gospel. An exhaustive list of the references in support of each theme can be found in Appendix 2. A separate chapter will conclude Part 2 by considering what John's Gospel contributes to our understanding of Jesus and the future. John does not include the Olivet Discourse but instead highlights the ways in which the results of Jesus' first coming are palpable already in the here and now while not neglecting the future dimension of Jesus's second coming.

Chapter 5

Persecution

Jesus regularly emphasized that the future would entail persecution for any who chose to commit their lives to him and embark on the journey of Christian discipleship. Future persecution is emphasized throughout the Gospels, likely indicating that the Gospel authors felt that Jesus' teaching about future persecution was particularly important for the early Christian communities. The first Christians (and Christians throughout history!) desperately needed to hear instructions from their Lord on how to view and endure persecution.[1] Jesus doesn't present future persecution as an "if" but as a "when." The predictions of persecution applied in the first instance to Jesus' first followers but pertain equally to his followers throughout history.

Matthew

Matthew 5:10–12

Matthew's first reference to persecution is found in Jesus' words in the Beatitudes. It is therefore important that we begin with this statement of Jesus as to what persecution is and what kind of reward awaits those who are persecuted. He says:

> [10] Blessed are those who are persecuted for righteousness' sake, for theirs is the kingdom of heaven. [11] Blessed are you when others revile you and persecute you and utter all kinds of evil against you falsely on my account. [12] Rejoice and be glad, for your reward is

---

1. Donald A. Hagner, *Matthew 1–13*, WBC 33A (Dallas: Word, 2002), 95.

great in heaven, for they persecuted the prophets who were before
you. (Matt 5:10–12)

Jesus knows that a time is going to come when those who follow him
will be persecuted and hated just like he himself was. One might even
say that the loyalty of these believers to God and his call upon their lives
becomes the cause of their further suffering. In this regard, as mentioned,
becoming a Christian makes life harder rather than easier.

Many people like to claim God's blessing upon their lives in the form
of financial provision and health, but few seem eager to embrace the blessedness associated with opposition and persecution. Jesus isn't telling us to
try to be persecuted, but he is preparing us for the inevitable and giving
us God's perspective. Despite how things might look from a human perspective, persecution and opposition for the sake of the gospel are signs
of God's favor and blessing. Jesus' words allow the divine perspective to
shape, mold, and transform our human perspectives.

Matthew 10:16–23, 24–25

The account of the commissioning of the disciples is the single longest
statement on persecution found in the Gospels. You can easily note similarities to Jesus' warnings in the Olivet Discourse.

> [16] Behold, I am sending you out as sheep in the midst of wolves,
> so be wise as serpents and innocent as doves. [17] Beware of men,
> for they will deliver you over to courts and flog you in their
> synagogues, [18] and you will be dragged before governors and
> kings for my sake, to bear witness before them and the Gentiles.
> [19] When they deliver you over, do not be anxious how you are
> to speak or what you are to say, for what you are to say will
> be given to you in that hour. [20] For it is not you who speak,
> but the Spirit of your Father speaking through you. [21] Brother
> will deliver brother over to death, and the father his child, and
> children will rise against parents and have them put to death,
> [22] and you will be hated by all for my name's sake. But the one
> who endures to the end will be saved. [23] When they persecute
> you in one town, flee to the next, for truly, I say to you, you will

not have gone through all the towns of Israel before the Son of Man comes.

Jesus begins with a warning to his disciples regarding the extent to which the world will reject them and their teachings. The reference to "sheep amidst wolves" indicates extreme danger and hostility. The serpent is normally used as a symbol of shrewdness and deception (Gen. 3:1) whereas a dove is used as a symbol of nobility and innocence (Hosea 7:11). One commentator writes, "The instructions are both practical (cf. the command to flee persecution, v. 23) and in keeping with the ethical tone of the teaching of Jesus. . . . Thus when in danger and in persecution, the disciples need practical discernment and at the same time the sort of guilelessness that characterized Jesus."[2]

The next warning is about the legal proceedings that will be central to the hostility meeting them. These legal proceedings will include physical punishments such as flogging. The disciples can expect to be delivered to courts and then to governors and kings to bear witness before the Jewish authorities and Gentiles. The use of "governor" is most likely a reference to Roman authorities.[3] Sham legal proceedings were common in the early persecution of the church and are common today in countries actively opposing the gospel.

Verses 19–20 come as important comfort to Jesus' followers. Jesus doesn't want them to be anxious about what they will say, for the Holy Spirit will provide all that is needed. The pouring out of God's Spirit signified a new era in God's plan and was a plain indication that the last days had begun (Acts 2:14–21). The Spirit is more commonly associated with Jesus in the Gospels, but here Jesus describes the Spirit as one who empowers and gives utterance to the disciples, not only Jesus himself.

Perhaps most disturbingly, there will be betrayals in families, and Jesus' followers will be hated by all because of his name. "Hated by all" here should not be taken to mean every human being but is a hyperbole to indicate widespread and strong opposition and hatred because of Jesus' name.[4]

---

2. Hagner, *Matthew 1–13*, 277.

3. Note the striking similarity with Jesus' journey to his death as he was first delivered to a Jewish council and then to the governor (Matt. 26:57–68; 27:1–2).

4. Leon Morris, *The Gospel according to Matthew*, PNTC (Grand Rapids: Eerdmans, 1992), 256.

As later in the Olivet Discourse, Jesus here promises that the one who endures to the end will be saved. What end is Jesus is referring to? Is he referring to the destruction of the temple in the year 70, the Parousia, the end of the persecution, the close of the age, or the very end of one's life? As we suggested regarding the Olivet Discourse, the "end" in this saying likely indicates each disciple's individual life. We each have the responsibility to endure unto the end; endurance to the end is not an optional add-on reserved only for super-spiritual people. Every believer will face opposition, and every believer must endure. Endurance is part and parcel of salvation in the same way that running a race is an essential part of winning a race. It is never sufficient simply to begin the race.

Jesus very practically and helpfully advises his followers to flee persecution. There is no need to try to get persecuted or try to find opposition; as we live faithfully, persecution will find us.[5] The ending of verse 23 has produced various interpretations because it indicates that Jesus' followers will not finish their journeys to all the towns of Israel before the Son of Man comes. The language of the coming of the Son of Man is drawn from Daniel 7:13–14 where the Son of Man comes to the Ancient of Days to receive dominion, glory, and a kingdom.

We noted in chapter 3 that Jesus and the earliest Christians interpreted and applied Daniel 7:13 to two separate events: (1) the ascension and enthronement of Jesus at God's right hand in heaven[6] and (2) Jesus' future visible and physical return to earth to establish his eternal kingdom.[7]

Those who think Matthew 10:23 is referring to Jesus' future second coming must interpret the reference to the disciples proclaiming the gospel to all the towns of Israel as a figurative way to describe the accomplishment of gospel proclamation to the Jewish people or, by extension, the worldwide proclamation of the gospel.[8] This is possible, but it is more natural

---

5. As Paul puts it in 2 Timothy 3:12, "Indeed, all who desire to live a godly life in Christ Jesus will be persecuted."

6. Matthew 10:23; 16:28; 26:64; Mark 14:62.

7. Matthew 13:40–41; 16:27; 25:31; Mark 8:38; Acts 1:11; 1 Corinthians 11:26; 15:23, 52; 1 Thessalonians 4:15; 2 Thessalonians 2:1; Titus 2:13; 2 Peter 3:4; Revelation 1:7; *Didache* 16:7–8.

8. Keener argues that Jesus is pointing to his future coming, for these persecutions would not come to an end any earlier: "Their missionary task and its attendant persecution would not be completed until Jesus' return . . . ; in the end, however, Israel would repent (23:39), just as the prophets had spoken (Deut. 4:30; Jer. 31:33; Ezek. 37:23; Hosea

here to connect this coming of the Son of Man with Jesus' ascension and enthronement at God's right hand. This makes better sense of the timing: Before Jesus' disciples could proclaim the gospel throughout Israel, he would be enthroned at God's right hand, exercising his rule and reign through the power of his Holy Spirit.

Why persecution? If Jesus is presently enthroned at God's right hand and ruling as the supreme King and Lord, why should his followers expect persecution at all? Jesus anticipates this problem and provides an answer in Matthew 10:24–25: "A disciple is not above his teacher, nor a servant above his master. It is enough for the disciple to be like his teacher, and the servant like his master. If they have called the master of the house Beelzebul, how much more will they malign those of his household."

Jesus explains that since he, their master and teacher, was persecuted and rejected, his followers should expect to experience the same. Jesus and his chosen disciples stand together; they are united. Following the suffering King will involve suffering as well: "Nevertheless, though these words are ominous, the disciples can be comforted that Jesus will have preceded them in the experience of suffering and rejection and in turn can sustain them in the midst of it. This has been the testimony of the church throughout the ages."[9]

Mark

Persecution is a prominent theme in Mark's Gospel. It is so important that some have called it definitive in the attempt to pinpoint the date of Mark.[10] The original readers of Mark's Gospel likely experienced some level of opposition and persecution as a present reality, and Jesus' words would have brought comfort and encouragement. The first hint of future persecution

---

2:14–23; 11:5–11; 14:1–7; Mal. 4:6)" (Craig S. Keener, *A Commentary on the Gospel of Matthew* [Grand Rapids: Eerdmans, 1999], 324).

9. Hagner, *Matthew 1–13*, 282.

10. James G. Crossley, *The Date of Mark's Gospel: Insight from the Law in Earliest Christianity*, JSNTSS 266 (London: T & T Clark, 2004), 79. Ralph Martin espoused the view that Mark was written in the light of a persecution (with reference to 8:34, 38; 10:30, 33, 45; 13: 8, 10 (cf. 1:14; 4:17; 6:17–29; 9:11–13, 30–32; 14:41), commenting, "These texts virtually speak for themselves and take on a deeper meaning when set in a background of a church which realizes its destiny as *ecclesia pressa* as the storm clouds of hostility from the Roman *imperium* gather" (Ralph P. Martin, *Mark: Evangelist and Theologian* [Grand Rapids: Zondervan, 1979], 66).

comes in the parable of the sower where Jesus describes some who receive the word and endure for a while but fall away when "tribulation or persecution arises on account of the word" (4:17).

Mark 8:34–38

The initial hint of coming persecution is confirmed in Jesus' ominous words in 8:34–38:

> [34] And calling the crowd to him with his disciples, he said to them, "If anyone would come after me, let him deny himself and take up his cross and follow me. [35] For whoever would save his life will lose it, but whoever loses his life for my sake and the gospel's will save it. [36] For what does it profit a man to gain the whole world and forfeit his soul? [37] For what can a man give in return for his soul? [38] For whoever is ashamed of me and of my words in this adulterous and sinful generation, of him will the Son of Man also be ashamed when he comes in the glory of his Father with the holy angels."

Who in their right mind would willingly follow Jesus if it involved taking up a cross? This doesn't mean, as some might think today, putting on a cross necklace or wearing a T-shirt with a cross on it. Jesus was inviting his original hearers to prepare for one of the most humiliating and painful executions used in the ancient world. It is at this point that Jesus is most unlike a salesman and certainly not behaving in a seeker-sensitive manner. He wanted his followers to be prepared for the worst, for he knew that some of them would in fact experience the worst. Those who truly believed in Jesus would follow him no matter what the cost, but for those who were wavering, Jesus' prediction of future suffering would gently push them toward the exit. No human definition of the good life involves carrying a cross to your own torture and execution. Jesus emphasizes, however, that such sacrifice and obedience were in fact the only way to truly attain life and to honor the Lord and Savior.

This message on persecution transitions into two of Jesus' other themes about the future discussed in the following chapters. Jesus describes his contemporaries as "this adulterous and sinful generation" and discusses the future coming of the Son of Man in glory with angels to bring judgment. Also, those who were presently ashamed of Jesus would not fare well in that future judgment, for Jesus would reciprocate their hesitancy to be identified with him and in return be ashamed of them.

Mark 10:28–31

> [28] Peter began to say to him, "See, we have left everything and followed you." [29] Jesus said, "Truly, I say to you, there is no one who has left house or brothers or sisters or mother or father or children or lands, for my sake and for the gospel, [30] who will not receive a hundredfold now in this time, houses and brothers and sisters and mothers and children and lands, with persecutions, and in the age to come eternal life. [31] But many who are first will be last, and the last first."

This saying also occurs in Matthew but Mark has an interesting additional element in the list of hundredfold blessings. God will bless his people in the present but the blessings would come "with persecutions." The persecutions are put into perspective by the next phrase: "in the age to come," God's people would receive eternal life. The logic here is similar to Paul's teaching in Romans 8:18: "For I consider that the sufferings of this present time are not worth comparing with the glory that is to be revealed to us."

Truth Touches Life: Your Response to Persecution

Persecution has been a reality throughout church history, but believers in different places and times don't experience it to the same degree. Depending upon where you live, you may not often think about persecution. How often does it cross your mind?

For those who are living in areas that are experiencing active and ongoing persecution, we encourage you and comfort you. Soldier on for Christ, stand strong, and remember our Savior's words: "Blessed are those who are persecuted for righteousness's sake, for theirs is the kingdom of heaven." In your circumstances, remember to bless those who persecute you and to pray for them, an attitude befitting true followers of our Lord and Savior.

For those who reside in places where persecution is not a problem, praise God! But you ought to be praying for those Christians living under persecution. Support the persecuted church in any way possible. Even as Paul urged the Colossian Christians to remember him in prison, we encourage Christians in safe places to heed the persecuted church's cry: "Remember my chains" (Col. 4:18).

Luke

As we've already seen in Matthew and Mark, Jesus predicts the future persecution that awaited his disciples. By warning of persecution, he calls on them to be strong and take courage, for whoever stands strong as a witness will receive a reward.

The first indication of future persecution comes in Luke's version of the Beatitudes where Jesus says, "Blessed are you when people hate you and when they exclude you and revile you and spurn your name as evil, on account of the Son of Man! Rejoice in that day, and leap for joy, for behold, your reward is great in heaven; for so their fathers did to the prophets" (Luke 6:22–23). Opposition and rejection because of our allegiance to Jesus should produce joy because it demonstrates our unity with God's past prophets who were persecuted and will result in future reward in heaven.

Luke's version of the parable of the sower indicates that those represented by the seeds on the rocks believe for a while but "in time of testing fall away" (8:13). Luke includes Jesus' call for his followers to take up their crosses and uniquely adds the adverb "daily" (9:23–25). Our embrace of sacrifice and suffering is not a one-time event but characterizes the entire journey of discipleship. In Luke's Gospel, Jesus speaks the most about persecution in chapter 12.[11]

Luke 12:1–12

This account parallels some of Jesus' teaching in the Olivet Discourse. This

---

11. A close study of this chapter has led Dennis Sweetland to conclude that "the gospel was composed in and for a time of persecution" ("Discipleship and Persecution: A Study of Luke 12, 1–12," *Biblica* 65 [1984]: 61).

likely indicates that Jesus spoke these words about future persecution on more than one occasion.

> [4] "I tell you, my friends, do not fear those who kill the body, and after that have nothing more that they can do. [5] But I will warn you whom to fear: fear him who, after he has killed, has authority to cast into hell. Yes, I tell you, fear him! [6] Are not five sparrows sold for two pennies? And not one of them is forgotten before God. [7] Why, even the hairs of your head are all numbered. Fear not; you are of more value than many sparrows."

After he warns the gathered crowd about the leaven of the Pharisees, Jesus changes the subject to believers' fate in this life and the life to come. By exhorting them "not to fear those who kill the body," Jesus is making two important points: (1) some of his followers will experience physical death because of persecution; and (2) physical death is not the end. Jesus doesn't want his disciples to be overcome by fear of what the immediate future will bring but rather to stay focused on the bigger picture, which includes the final judgment at the end of the age, punishment in hell, and resurrection life in God's kingdom.[12] This is the greater prize to which the eyes of Jesus' followers should look.

Those who harm the body and then are incapable of doing anything else should be understood as their potential persecutors. Jesus stops short of promising his disciples that he'll save them from physical death but assures them that there's no way their persecutors will be able to touch their souls (using Matthew's language in 10:28).[13] Physical death can very well be part of their journey of discipleship as they daily carry their crosses.

Jesus focuses again on persecution a few verses later.

> [11] "And when they bring you before the synagogues and the rulers and the authorities, do not be anxious about how you should

---

12. Sweetland, "Discipleship and Persecution," 69.

13. These words of Jesus are reminiscent of his reply to Pilate when Pilate wrongly thinks that he has power over Jesus. Jesus corrects him saying: "You would have no authority over me at all unless it had been given you from above" (John 19:11).

defend yourself or what you should say, [12] for the Holy Spirit will teach you in that very hour what you ought to say."

This is the section that is rather close to the Olivet Discourse. Earlier, Jesus spoke of the dangers that awaited the disciples; now he speaks with certainty of a time when they will be brought before synagogues, rulers, and authorities to give "a defense for their hope" to use a phrase from Peter (1 Peter 3:15). Jesus comforts his disciples with the assurance that the Holy Spirit will teach them what to say. They will not be alone! As one scholar notes,

> Jesus' teaching on persecution in Luke 12 can be summarized as follows: "The danger facing the disciples is apostasy for which there will be no forgiveness (12:10). Although this danger is very real, the faithful disciple is told not to be anxious, for God will provide ultimate protection (11:13; 12:12, 22f.). Indeed, the appropriate response of the faithful disciples to persecution is joy (cf. 6:22f.; Acts 13:30ff.) because their names are written in heaven (10:20) and God wants to give them the kingdom (12:32)."[14]

Summary: Persecution Is Coming

Jesus' teaching about future persecution is both clear and mind-boggling. He tells his followers in advance that they will likely experience terrible suffering for their allegiance to him but that it will all be worth it in the end. Persecution exposes our deepest beliefs. Do we really believe that the sufferings of this present time are not worth comparing with the future glory of eternal life with Jesus in the new heavens and new earth? Many Christians may confidently think that they will be faithful to God no matter what the cost. They may think that no amount of pain, loss, or torture would lead them to renounce Christ. Such confidence seems quite a bit like Peter's confidence that he would never deny Jesus the night he was betrayed (and we all know how that turned out!).

A reliable guide to our decisions in possible future moments of persecution are our daily decisions in the present. Are you taking up your cross daily to follow Jesus now? Do you regularly and willingly make small

---

14. Sweetland, "Discipleship and Persecution," 79.

sacrifices because of your allegiance to Jesus? Are you actively seeking to make Jesus Lord over every aspect of your life day by day in the present? If so, then there is little to fear regarding future persecution. If not, however, no amount of present confidence will be able to prepare you for the worst.

Chapter 6

Growing Conflict, Rejection, and the Judgment of Jerusalem

In the next chapter, we will consider what Jesus taught about his future coming as the Son of Man in the final judgment at the end of history as we know it. This focus on Jesus' future coming, however, often causes readers to miss the developing conflict Jesus experienced with the Jewish religious leaders and the judgment he prophesied against them in the imminent future.

We noted in Part 1 that Jesus at the beginning of the Olivet Discourse prophesied the destruction of the temple and Jerusalem which took place in the year 70. Jesus' pronouncement at the beginning of the Olivet Discourse is not an isolated incident but the culmination of a trajectory of growing conflict and rejection of Jesus by the leaders of his own people.

Jesus' continued references to "this generation" as well as his growing conflict with the Jewish leaders prepare the way for his climactic discussion in the Olivet Discourse of the destruction of the temple and Jerusalem within the lifetime of his original hearers. In Part 1, we briefly discussed "this generation"; now it will be helpful to look at the passages in more detail.

Matthew: This Generation

Matthew 11:16–19

> 16 But to what shall I compare *this generation*? It is like children sitting in the marketplaces and calling to their playmates, 17 "We played the flute for you, and you did not dance; we sang a dirge,

and you did not mourn." [18] For John came neither eating nor drinking, and they say, "He has a demon." [19] The Son of Man came eating and drinking, and they say, "Look at him! A glutton and a drunkard, a friend of tax collectors and sinners!" Yet wisdom is justified by her deeds.

In the Gospels, references to "this generation" always carry negative connotations of disobedience, unbelief, and rejection. In this first occurrence of the phrase, Jesus chooses a rather unusual analogy to describe the current generation. People were like two groups of children in a market. One group played a flute—as in a wedding—for the other group while the other group refused to dance. As if that weren't enough, the first group played a dirge—as in a funeral song—and the other group refused to respond in the natural way by way of mourning. No matter what the one group of children did, the other group wouldn't go along:

> In a similar way, the present generation (i.e., of Jesus' contemporaries) will have nothing to do with the messengers sent to them by God. Thus the simile actually likens the unbelief of the present generation to the children who flatly refuse to participate in anything offered to them.[1]

Like children who refuse to play with others, "this generation" found it easier to ignore what was going on around them. John the Baptist stepped away from normal life to lead an ascetic lifestyle and was accused of demon possession whereas Jesus who came eating and drinking was accused of gluttony, drunkenness, and friendship with sinners and tax collectors. "This generation" both rejected the forerunner to the Messiah and was in the process of rejecting the Messiah himself. In effect, Jesus says:

> But all you do is to give orders and criticize. For you the Baptist is a madman because he fasts, while you want to make merry; me you reproach because I eat with publicans, while you insist on strict separation from sinners. You hate the preaching of repentance,

---

1. Donald A. Hagner, *Matthew 1–13*, WBC 33A (Dallas: Word, 2002), 310.

and you hate the proclamation of the gospel. So you play your childish game with God's messengers while Rome burns![2]

Matthew 12:38–45

[38] Then some of the scribes and Pharisees answered him, saying, "Teacher, we wish to see a sign from you." [39] But he answered them, *"An evil and adulterous generation* seeks for a sign, but no sign will be given to it except the sign of the prophet Jonah. [40] For just as Jonah was three days and three nights in the belly of the great fish, so will the Son of Man be three days and three nights in the heart of the earth. [41] The men of Nineveh will rise up at the judgment with *this generation* and condemn it, for they repented at the preaching of Jonah, and behold, something greater than Jonah is here. [42] The queen of the South will rise up at the judgment with *this generation* and condemn it, for she came from the ends of the earth to hear the wisdom of Solomon, and behold, something greater than Solomon is here.

[43] When the unclean spirit has gone out of a person, it passes through waterless places seeking rest, but finds none. [44] Then it says, 'I will return to my house from which I came.' And when it comes, it finds the house empty, swept, and put in order. [45] Then it goes and brings with it seven other spirits more evil than itself, and they enter and dwell there, and the last state of that person is worse than the first. So also will it be with *this evil generation."*

The Jewish leaders approach Jesus demanding a sign that would prove conclusively that Jesus was who he claimed to be. Jesus retorts by calling them an "evil and adulterous generation."[3] This may seem harsh of Jesus.

---

2. D. A. Carson, "Matthew," in *The Expositor's Bible Commentary*, rev. ed., ed. Tremper Longman III and David E. Garland, vol. 9: *Matthew and Mark* (Grand Rapids: Zondervan, 2010), 313, citing Joachim Jeremias, *The Parables of Jesus*, trans. S. H. Hooke (London: SCM, 1963), 161–62.

3. See Carson, "Matthew," 340: "'Adultery' was frequently used by Old Testament prophets to describe the spiritual prostitution and wanton apostasy of Israel (e.g., Isa. 50:1; 57:3; Jer. 3:8; 13:27; 31:32; Ezek. 16:15, 32, 35–42; Hosea 2:1–7; 3:1). . . . Israel had largely abandoned her idolatry and syncretism after the exile. But now Jesus insists that she was still adulterous in heart. In the past God had graciously granted 'signs' to strengthen the faith of the timid (e.g., Abraham [Gen. 15]; Gideon [Judg. 6:17–24]; Joshua [Josh. 10])."

Why would he respond in such a way? Pharisees and scribes had been present at some of Jesus' miracles throughout his ministry and had doubtless heard eyewitness accounts of other miracles. Somehow Jesus knew that no sign would convince these leaders that he was the Messiah—no sign, that is, except the sign of Jonah. Jesus refers to the sign of Jonah typologically to describe his own death and resurrection, which had not yet taken place. Just as Jonah was rescued from the belly of the fish after three days and went on to proclaim God's message to Nineveh, Jesus would escape death through resurrection. Yet Jesus' preaching would be attested by a deliverance even greater than that of Jonah: bodily resurrection.

Jesus further describes this evil and adulterous generation by comparing it to a person from whom an evil spirit had been exorcised but who was promptly repossessed by seven additional spirits more powerful that the first. In the end, the person was worse off than when possessed by only one spirit. Jesus used this illustration in response to the unbelief and resistance he was encountering from the Jewish religious leaders. Based on the context, the analogy is easy to understand. The current generation had already experienced the powerful deeds of Jesus, including demon exorcism. However, this evil and adulterous generation had not shown any repentance or commitment to Jesus but rather continued to reject and oppose him. Therefore, despite Jesus' powerful proclamation and miracles, the current generation was as susceptible to the power of evil as ever; indeed, the judgment it would experience would be far worse than when Jesus began his ministry. Judgment was on the horizon.

Matthew 16:1–4

[1] And the Pharisees and Sadducees came, and to test him they asked him to show them a sign from heaven. [2] He answered them, "When it is evening, you say, 'It will be fair weather, for the sky is red.' [3] And in the morning, 'It will be stormy today, for the sky is red and threatening.' You know how to interpret the appearance of the sky, but you cannot interpret the signs of the times. [4] *An evil and adulterous generation* seeks for a sign, but no sign will be given to it except the sign of Jonah." So he left them and departed.

Here, however, Jesus says that signs are denied 'this wicked and adulterous generation,' because they are never to be performed on demand or as a sop to unbelief (cf. 1 Cor. 1:22)."

Later in Jesus' ministry, the Pharisees again seek a sign, this time accompanied by their political rivals, the Sadducees. Matthew is clearer the second time and comments on their motives: They were trying to test Jesus. These leaders didn't come with humility and genuine interest but to try to trick Jesus into doing or saying something they could use against him.

Jesus answers by contrasting their ability to read signs associated with weather with their inability to interpret the signs of the times. As earlier in Matthew 12:38–42, Jesus refuses to give them any other sign apart from that of Jonah. Jesus thus rebukes these leaders as the epitome of an evil and adulterous generation—a generation that continually fails to recognize that Jesus himself is the ultimate sign from God.

Matthew 17:14–18

> [14] And when they came to the crowd, a man came up to him and, kneeling before him, [15] said, "Lord, have mercy on my son, for he is an epileptic and he suffers terribly. For often he falls into the fire, and often into the water. [16] And I brought him to your disciples, and they could not heal him." [17] And Jesus answered, "O faithless and twisted generation, how long am I to be with you? How long am I to bear with you? Bring him here to me." [18] And Jesus rebuked the demon, and it came out of him, and the boy was healed instantly.

Jesus' reference to the current "faithless and twisted generation" is triggered by his disciples' lack of faith. The critique, however, cannot be limited to the disciples and uses their lack of faith to critique the current generation, which was generally characterized by a lack of faith. In this regard, the disciples were representative of and a product of their generation.

Matthew: Conflict Parables

Tuesday of Jesus' final week was a day of conflict. The day began with the Jewish leaders confronting Jesus about his actions of cleansing the temple the previous day. They were upset and rightly viewed Jesus' actions as a challenge to their own authority. Jesus responded by telling three conflict parables transparently directed against the Jewish leadership. These parables don't include the phrase "this generation" but are an important part of the theme and build toward Jesus' climactic statement at the end of that same day (Tuesday) that the temple would be destroyed within the lifetime of his contemporaries.

The first parable describes the current Jewish leaders as a son who agreed to work in his father's vineyard but then refused to go (Matt. 21:28–32). This parable is found only in Matthew's Gospel. Jesus concludes the parable by noting, "The tax collectors and the prostitutes go into the kingdom of God before you. For John came to you in the way of righteousness, and you did not believe him, but the tax collectors and the prostitutes believed him. And even when you saw it, you did not afterward change your minds and believe him" (Matt. 21:31–32). The very suggestion that tax collectors and prostitutes were more favored by God than the current religious leaders would have deeply offended them, but Jesus isn't concerned about protecting their feelings. They hadn't responded with repentance and obedience to God's will while many of the most sinful and marginalized in the society had shown signs of repentance.

The second parable describes the Jewish leaders as tenants who had been put in charge of God's vineyard, Israel (Matt. 21:33–46).[4] The tenants beat, kill, and stone the vineyard owner's messengers and eventually even kill his son to take the vineyard for themselves. Jesus allows his hearers to complete the story for him: "When therefore the owner of the vineyard comes, what will he do to those tenants?" (Matt. 21:40). Jesus' listeners responded with more prophetic insight than they probably realized at the time: "They said to him, 'He will put those wretches to a miserable death and let out the vineyard to other tenants who will give him the fruits in their seasons'" (Matt. 21:41). Jesus affirms their answer and squarely addresses the religious leaders: "Therefore I tell you, the kingdom of God will be taken away from you and given to a people producing its fruits" (Matt. 21:43). This is a truly astounding statement: The kingdom of God had been closely associated with the ethnic people of Israel throughout the Old Testament but it would soon be torn away from this ethnic connection and given to a people who would produce the fruit of the kingdom. Jesus' point was not lost on the Jewish leaders who renewed their attempts to trap and arrest him: "When the chief priests

---

4. In Isaiah 5:1–7, Isaiah described Israel as God's unproductive vineyard which would soon be judged. Jesus seems to build on this passage in his parable but pins guilt on the current Jewish leadership, the tenants.

and the Pharisees heard his parables, they perceived that he was speaking about them" (Matt. 21:45).

Jesus didn't stop there but told a third parable in which a king gave a wedding feast for his son and sent servants to call everyone who had been invited to the wedding (Matt. 22:1–14). Some of those invited ignored the invitation while others scandalously abused and killed the messengers, an open act of defiance against the king. The king responded in two ways. First, "he sent his troops and destroyed those murderers and burned their city" (Matt. 22:7). Second, he sent his servants to invite anyone they could find to his son's wedding feast. With this parable, Jesus prepares for his pronouncement later in the day that the temple and Jerusalem will be destroyed. The Jewish people, represented by their religious leaders, had rejected God's messengers and refused his invitation to the kingdom.

These three conflict parables prepare the way for Matthew 23 where Jesus stops using parables and speaks directly in judgment against the present generation.

Matthew 23:32–39

32 Fill up, then, the measure of your fathers. 33 You serpents, you brood of vipers, how are you to escape being sentenced to hell? 34 Therefore I send you prophets and wise men and scribes, some of whom you will kill and crucify, and some you will flog in your synagogues and persecute from town to town, 35 so that on you may come all the righteous blood shed on earth, from the blood of righteous Abel to the blood of Zechariah the son of Barachiah, whom you murdered between the sanctuary and the altar. 36 Truly, I say to you, all these things will come upon *this generation*. 37 "O Jerusalem, Jerusalem, the city that kills the prophets and stones those who are sent to it! How often would I have gathered your children together as a hen gathers her brood under her wings, and you were not willing! 38 See, your house is left to you desolate. 39 For I tell you, you will not see me again, until you say, 'Blessed is he who comes in the name of the Lord.'"

Matthew 23 is a long and disturbing chapter consisting of seven woes spoken by Jesus against the scribes and Pharisees. Most of Jesus' critique throughout the chapter focuses on the hypocrisy of the Jewish religious leaders. There are parallels to some parts of this chapter scattered throughout Mark and Luke, but nothing elsewhere in the four Gospels comes close to equaling the scale and severity of Jesus' critique in Matthew 23. Jesus was engaging in a verbal and rhetorical war with the current Jewish religious leadership for the hearts and minds of the common people. The chapter concludes with Jesus mourning over Jerusalem and the fact that her house, the temple, would soon be left desolate. It is no accident that this chapter transitions directly into Jesus' prophecy of the temple's destruction at the beginning of the Olivet Discourse in Matthew 24.

The coming destruction of Jerusalem is explicitly described as judgment for the unwillingness of the current generation to recognize God's activity among them and for their hostility and opposition to Jesus which Jesus knew would culminate in his death.[5]

Mark

The growing conflict between Jesus and the Jewish religious leaders runs like a thread through Mark's Gospel. On Jesus' side, it culminates in his teaching in the Olivet Discourse about the judgment and destruction of the temple, whereas on the side of the religious leaders it culminates in their success in orchestrating Jesus' crucifixion. As we saw in Matthew's Gospel, this is a major theme even though it is often overlooked by modern readers because it is ancient history to us and doesn't seem quite as applicable to our present situation. It was certainly important to Jesus and his first followers!

The conflict in Mark starts slowly and grows in intensity as the Gospel progresses. The first indication that Jesus and the Jewish religious leaders were moving in different directions comes when they question Jesus' disciples about why he ate with tax collectors and sinners (2:16–17). This is certainly not something a righteous man and up-and-coming young rabbi should be doing. More seriously, the Pharisees later confronted Jesus for the way in which his disciples were breaking the laws of the Sabbath by plucking and snacking on heads of grain in a field. Jesus boldly responds by declaring his lordship, as the Son of Man, over the Sabbath (2:23–28).

---

5. Jesus predicted his own death and resurrection (Matt. 16:21; 17:9, 12, 22–23; 20:17–19; 26:2, 12; and parallels in Mark and Luke).

Chapter 3 begins with people suspiciously watching Jesus to see if he is going to heal on the Sabbath, which he promptly does (3:1–6). Mark indicates that this incident produced both anger and grief in Jesus, and the Pharisees, along with the Herodians, began plotting his demise. The first serious attempt to discredit Jesus came with attempts to associate him with evil powers: "And the scribes who came down from Jerusalem were saying, 'He is possessed by Beelzebul,' and 'by the prince of demons he casts out the demons'" (3:22). Jesus responds by associating their accusations with blasphemy against the Holy Spirit, an unforgiveable sin. Jesus also responds by switching his teaching style to focus more on parables as an act of judgment against those who were opposing him. Parables ensure that those without understanding remain in a state of ignorance.

Mark 7:6–13

> [6] And he said to them, "Well did Isaiah prophesy of you hypocrites, as it is written, 'This people honors me with their lips, but their heart is far from me; [7] in vain do they worship me, teaching as doctrines the commandments of men.' [8] You leave the commandment of God and hold to the tradition of men." [9] And he said to them, "You have a fine way of rejecting the commandment of God in order to establish your tradition! [10] For Moses said, 'Honor your father and your mother'; and, 'Whoever reviles father or mother must surely die.' [11] But you say, 'If a man tells his father or his mother, "Whatever you would have gained from me is Corban"' (that is, given to God)— [12] then you no longer permit him to do anything for his father or mother, [13] thus making void the word of God by your tradition that you have handed down. And many such things you do."

Jesus utters this critique in response to the question from the Pharisees and scribes about why Jesus' disciples eat with ceremonially unclean hands. Although taking place earlier in his ministry, this critique shares several elements with the seven woes of Matthew 23 discussed above. Jesus accuses them of being hypocrites who abandon the commandments of God to enforce the commandments and traditions of men. At this point in Mark's narrative, the adversarial relationship between Jesus and the Jewish religious leaders is quite entrenched and obvious to all.

Mark 8:11–13

> [11] The Pharisees came and began to argue with him, seeking from him a sign from heaven to test him. [12] And he sighed deeply in his spirit and said, "Why does this generation seek a sign? Truly, I say to you, no sign will be given to this generation." [13] And he left them, got into the boat again, and went to the other side.

This account is shorter than the parallel we looked at in Matthew in the previous chapter. Mark's account is more concise and highlights Jesus' frustration with "this generation." The Pharisees weren't genuinely seeking a sign motivated by faith; they had already rejected his authority. In Mark, Jesus flatly refuses to give them any sign, and his abrupt departure conveys judgment.

Mark 8:38

> [38] If anyone is ashamed of me and my words in this adulterous and sinful generation, the Son of Man will be ashamed of him when he comes in his Father's glory with the holy angels.

Jesus follows up his refusal to give a sign to "this generation" with a description of it as "adulterous and sinful." God often charged Israel with the sin of adultery in the Old Testament. Adultery and unfaithfulness are main themes in the message of Hosea while God divorces Israel because of her adulterous acts in Jeremiah 3:8. France notes the connection between Israel in the Old Testament and this generation:

> Μοιχαλίς (adultery) expresses the frequent charge in OT prophecy that Israel is committing adultery against God, her true husband; "this generation" is thus characterized as a whole as in rebellion against God and therefore also against his Messiah. The polarization assumed in these verses marks a more pessimistic assessment than was found in most of the Galilean phase of the story, and points forward rather to the confrontation in Jerusalem.[6]

---

6. France, *Gospel of Mark*, 342.

Mark 9:19

> [19] And he answered them, "O faithless generation, how long am I to be with you? How long am I to bear with you? Bring him to me."

The context and pronouncement is comparable to what we saw in Matthew's Gospel. Jesus utters this statement in response to the inability of his disciples to cast out a demon but Jesus seems to be focusing more broadly on the entire current generation of which his disciples were representative.

The Fig Tree (Mark 11:12–22)

> [12] On the following day, when they came from Bethany, he was hungry. [13] And seeing in the distance a fig tree in leaf, he went to see if he could find anything on it. When he came to it, he found nothing but leaves, *for it was not the season for figs.* [14] And he said to it, "May no one ever eat fruit from you again." And his disciples heard it.
>
> [15] And they came to Jerusalem. And he entered the temple and began to drive out those who sold and those who bought in the temple, and he overturned the tables of the money-changers and the seats of those who sold pigeons. [16] And he would not allow anyone to carry anything through the temple. [17] And he was teaching them and saying to them, "Is it not written, 'My house shall be called a house of prayer for all the nations'? But you have made it a den of robbers." [18] And the chief priests and the scribes heard it and were seeking a way to destroy him, for they feared him, because all the crowd was astonished at his teaching. [19] And when evening came they went out of the city.
>
> [20] As they passed by in the morning, they saw the fig tree withered away to its roots. [21] And Peter remembered and said to him, "Rabbi, look! The fig tree that you cursed has withered."

Many readers have been puzzled by Jesus' action in cursing the fig tree during the final week of his life. Jesus was hungry on Monday morning while walking from Bethany to Jerusalem and saw a fig tree in the distance with leaves on it. When he arrives and doesn't find anything worth eating, he curses the fig tree. On the next day, the disciples notice that the fig tree has withered, and Peter remembers how Jesus had cursed it.

Some interpreters try to explain Jesus' actions by noting that by the time a fig tree has leaves, it also has small unripe figs on it that could be eaten prematurely if anyone were very hungry. Also, if there are no signs of initial fruit by the time the tree has leaves, there will be no harvest later. These things are true enough but miss the point in Mark's narrative because Mark—alone among the Gospel authors—makes the explicit point that it was not the season for figs. This comment by Mark has further confused readers. Why would Jesus curse a fig tree for not having fruit at a time of the year when its fruit would not even be ripe? Was he just hungry and grumpy? Contrary to this preposterous idea, Mark's comment, "It was not the season for figs," was a way for him to alert the reader to the fact that Jesus' curse was not about the figs or the fig tree. There was something more important going on. This suspicion is confirmed by the way in which Mark's narrative splits his discussion of the fig tree over the course of two days with an event in the middle: the cleansing of the temple in Jerusalem (something scholars refer to playfully as a "Markan sandwich").

The temple, the main symbol of Judaism and center of worship and devotion to God, had become corrupt. It had ceased to function as a house of prayer for all the nations but had instead become a cave of robbers. Jesus cleansed the temple as an act of judgment against it and the Jewish religious leadership. Two further observations confirm the idea that Jesus' cursing of the fig tree should be connected to the cleansing of the temple. First, the fig tree was often used as a symbol for Israel in the Old Testament.[7]

Second, many of the Old Testament prophets engaged in symbolic acts to convey their message of judgment. When reading Jeremiah and Ezekiel, you will be struck by the strange nature of some of these acted-out parables. The cursing of the fig tree by Jesus is an acted-out parable of judgment that Jesus performed immediately before he entered Jerusalem to cleanse the temple while serving at the same time as an action communicating God's judgment on the corruption of the religious leaders.

By using the story of the fig tree to sandwich the account of the cleansing of the temple, Mark makes clear that it was an acted-out parable

---

7. Hosea 9:10; Jeremiah 24:1–10; Joel 1:7.

of judgment against Israel because her worship had been corrupted and the religious leaders were by and large rejecting God's Messiah. There was still time for repentance but that time was short. Historically, time ran out in the year 70 when Roman armies destroyed Jerusalem and the temple.

A Conflict Parable (Mark 12:1–12)

While Matthew contains three conflict parables spoken by Jesus against the religious leaders during his final week, Mark contains only one, arguably the most damning, the parable of the tenants. The details are comparable to those in Matthew, and the religious leaders "perceived that he had told the parable against them" (12:12). One aspect of the parable is more severe in Mark than in Matthew. In Matthew, Jesus asks the people what the vineyard owner would do to the tenants, while Mark records a quick and direct statement from Jesus about their fate: "He will come and destroy the tenants and give the vineyard to others" (Mark 12:9). This anticipates Jesus' prophecy of the temple's destruction at the beginning of the Olivet Discourse later that day.

Beware of the Scribes (Mark 12:38–40)

[38] And in his teaching he said, "Beware of the scribes, who like to walk around in long robes and like greetings in the marketplaces [39] and have the best seats in the synagogues and the places of honor at feasts, [40] who devour widows' houses and for a pretense make long prayers. They will receive the greater condemnation."

Mark has nothing corresponding to the devastating critique of the seven woes in Matthew 23 but does include these short sayings against the scribes. Jesus highlights several elements that reveal their hypocrisy and flatly states that "they will receive the greater condemnation."

Luke

Luke follows Mark quite closely in the development of conflict between Jesus and the Jewish religious leaders but includes more material and focuses even more than Mark on the coming judgment of the year 70. Based on our discussion up to this point in the chapter, the following verses in Luke should be self-explanatory.

Growing Conflict in Luke

• "And the scribes and the Pharisees began to question, saying, 'Who is this who speaks blasphemies? Who can forgive sins but God alone?'" (Luke 5:21).

• "And the Pharisees and their scribes grumbled at his disciples, saying, 'Why do you eat and drink with tax collectors and sinners?'" (Luke 5:30).

• "But some of the Pharisees said, 'Why are you doing what is not lawful to do on the Sabbath?'" (Luke 6:2).

• "And the scribes and the Pharisees watched him, to see whether he would heal on the Sabbath, so that they might find a reason to accuse him" (Luke 6:7).

• "(But the Pharisees and the lawyers rejected the purpose of God for themselves, not having been baptized by him [John].) 'To what then shall I compare the people of this generation, and what are they like? They are like children sitting in the marketplace and calling to one another, "We played the flute for you, and you did not dance; we sang a dirge, and you did not weep." For John the Baptist has come eating no bread and drinking no wine, and you say, "He has a demon." The Son of Man has come eating and drinking, and you say, "Look at him! A glutton and a drunkard, a friend of tax collectors and sinners!" Yet wisdom is justified by all her children'" (Luke 7:30–35).

• "'And I begged your disciples to cast it out, but they could not.' Jesus answered, 'O faithless and twisted generation, how long am I to be with you and bear with you? Bring your son here'" (Luke 9:40–41).

• "Woe to you, Chorazin! Woe to you, Bethsaida! For if the mighty works done in you had been done in Tyre and Sidon, they would have repented long ago, sitting in sackcloth and ashes. But it will be more bearable in the judgment for Tyre and Sidon than for you. And you, Capernaum, will you be exalted to heaven? You shall be brought down to Hades" (Luke 10:13–15).

• "But some of them said, 'He casts out demons by Beelzebul, the prince of demons,' while others, to test him, kept seeking from him a sign from heaven" (Luke 11:15–16).

• "When the crowds were increasing, he began to say, 'This generation is an evil generation. It seeks for a sign, but no sign will be given to it except the sign of Jonah. For as Jonah became a sign to the people of Nineveh, so will the Son of Man be to this generation. The queen of the South will rise up at the judgment with the men of this generation and condemn them, for she came from the ends of the earth to hear the wisdom of Solomon, and behold, something greater than Solomon is here. The men of Nineveh will rise up at the judgment with this generation and condemn it, for they repented at the preaching of Jonah, and behold, something greater than Jonah is here" (Luke 11:29–32).

• "Beware of the leaven of the Pharisees, which is hypocrisy" (Luke 12:1).

• "But the ruler of the synagogue, indignant because Jesus had healed on the Sabbath, said to the people, 'There are six days in which work ought to be done. Come on those days and be healed, and not on the Sabbath day'" (Luke 13:14).

• "Now the tax collectors and sinners were all drawing near to hear him. And the Pharisees and the scribes grumbled, saying, 'This man receives sinners and eats with them'" (Luke 15:1–2).

• "The Pharisees, who were lovers of money, heard all these things, and they ridiculed him. And he said to them, 'You are those who justify yourselves before men, but God knows your hearts. For what is exalted among men is an abomination in the sight of God'" (Luke 16:14–15).

• "And in the hearing of all the people he said to his disciples, 'Beware of the scribes, who like to walk around in long robes, and love greetings in the marketplaces and the best seats in the synagogues and the places of honor at feasts, who devour widows' houses and for a pretense make long prayers. They will receive the greater condemnation'" (Luke 20:45–47).

In addition to these sayings shared with either Matthew or Mark, Luke contains several unique passages related to the judgment of the year 70.

John the Baptist

Although technically beyond the scope of our focus on Jesus' teaching about the future, John the Baptist makes several comments concerning the judgment that would be associated with Jesus and his ministry.

> [8] Bear fruits in keeping with repentance. And do not begin to say to yourselves, "We have Abraham as our father." For I tell you, God is able from these stones to raise up children for Abraham. [9] Even now the axe is laid to the root of the trees. Every tree therefore that does not bear good fruit is cut down and thrown into the fire. . . . [17] His [Jesus'] winnowing fork is in his hand, to clear his threshing floor and to gather the wheat into his barn, but the chaff he will burn with unquenchable fire. (Luke 3:8–9, 17)

John calls people to repentance for the sole reason that judgment is on the horizon; the axe is already swinging against the root of the trees. John stresses that in this coming judgment ethnicity won't be enough to save people from punishment since God could raise up children for Abraham from stones (another hyperbole). John proceeds to connect this judgment with Jesus and his coming. This could be referring to the final judgment, but John's stress on imminence more readily seems to indicate the judgment of the year 70. That present generation was a generation of crisis.

Woes to the Pharisees and Lawyers (Luke 11:37–54)

Luke's Gospel doesn't contain the lengthy seven woes of Matthew 23 but does include similar material in a heated exchange between Jesus, a Pharisee, and a lawyer. Jesus upbraids these individuals for their hypocrisy, pride, and arrogance. His chastisement culminates in the declaration that the current generation will be held accountable for the nations' rejection of God's messengers.

> [49] Therefore also the Wisdom of God said, "I will send them prophets and apostles, some of whom they will kill and persecute," [50] so that the blood of all the prophets, shed from the foundation of the

world, may be charged against this generation, [51] from the blood
of Abel to the blood of Zechariah, who perished between the altar
and the sanctuary. Yes, I tell you, it will be required of this generation. (Luke 11:49–51)

Jesus unapologetically singled out the current generation as the generation of accountability. They were in the process of rejecting God's own Son
and would soon kill him. Jesus' death would be the culmination of the trajectory evident in their rejection of God's messengers in the Old Testament.
Judgment, however, was coming. The scribes and Pharisees went away from
this encounter with a renewed desire to trap him in his words.

Parables of Judgment

Luke shares the Parable of the Tenants with both Matthew and Mark
(Luke 20:9–18). The fate of the evil tenants matches that described in the
other Gospels: "He will come and destroy those tenants and give the vineyard to others" (Luke 20:16). Unlike Matthew and Mark, Luke doesn't
note that the religious leaders perceived the parable as having been spoken
against them, but Luke likely felt that its meaning was transparent. God
will judge the current religious leaders for mismanaging his vineyard and
killing his Son.

Luke also shares the Parable of the Great Banquet with Matthew (Luke
14:15–24). Luke's version is slightly different, but the main point is the
same. Those originally invited to the banquet made excuses and refused
to come, so the master issued an open invitation and sent his servants to
gather all who would come but "none of those men who were invited shall
taste my banquet" (Luke 14:24).

Laments over Jerusalem

One of Luke's laments is shared with Matthew but the other two are
unique to his Gospel. These laments focus specifically on the destruction
of Jerusalem and the temple in the year 70. Luke's first lament comes in
13:34–35 as Jesus journeys toward Jerusalem for the final week of his
earthly life:

[34] O Jerusalem, Jerusalem, the city that kills the prophets and
stones those who are sent to it! How often would I have gathered

your children together as a hen gathers her brood under her wings, and you were not willing! [35] Behold, your house is forsaken. And I tell you, you will not see me until you say, "Blessed is he who comes in the name of the Lord!"

The passage parallels Jesus' lament at the end of the seven woes of Matthew 23:37–39. As in Matthew, Jesus mourns Jerusalem's lack of response and declares that "the house"—the temple—was forsaken. This is followed in Luke by an even more specific lament spoken by Jesus amid his triumphal entry on Sunday at the beginning of the last week of his life:

> [41] And when he drew near and saw the city, he wept over it, [42] saying, "Would that you, even you, had known on this day the things that make for peace! But now they are hidden from your eyes. [43] For the days will come upon you, when your enemies will set up a barricade around you and surround you and hem you in on every side [44] and tear you down to the ground, you and your children within you. And they will not leave one stone upon another in you, because you did not know the time of your visitation." (Luke 19:41–44)

The only other place where we're told that Jesus weeps is at the death of his friend Lazarus (John 11:35). Jesus very specifically describes the judgment that will soon come upon Jerusalem—it will be destroyed. This prophecy focuses on Jerusalem itself and so differs from the prophecy about the destruction of the temple at the beginning of the Olivet Discourse. The two prophecies are related, and the destruction of one entailed the destruction of the other.

Finally, after Simon of Cyrene takes Jesus' cross on the way to the crucifixion, Jesus makes the following comments to women who are mourning for him and for his fate:

> [28] But turning to them Jesus said, "Daughters of Jerusalem, do not weep for me, but weep for yourselves and for your children. [29] For behold, the days are coming when they will say, 'Blessed are the barren and the wombs that never bore and the breasts that never nursed!' [30] Then they will begin to say to the mountains, 'Fall

on us,' and to the hills, 'Cover us.' [31] For if they do these things when the wood is green, what will happen when it is dry?" (Luke 23:28–31)

Even as people are mourning over him, he attempts to redirect their mourning toward their own fate because he knows what lies ahead for Jerusalem and its people. He had already very specifically predicted the destruction of both Jerusalem and her temple within the lifetime of that current generation, so he knew what terror lay ahead for the nation that had rejected him and his message. Jesus' words here climax the conflict between him and the religious leaders, which resulted in his journey down the Via Dolorosa. This evil and adulterous generation had pushed the Messiah all the way to the cross, and now judgment wasn't too far off; for to reject the Messiah is to set oneself against God.

Conclusion: The Destruction of Jerusalem and the Temple

It may seem strange for us to spend time looking at Jesus' conflicts with the Jewish religious leaders in a book about Jesus' teaching on the future, but these conflicts are foundational for understanding Jesus' pronouncements of judgment that were fulfilled in the destruction of Jerusalem in the year 70. Jesus' pronouncement and discussion of the temple's destruction in the Olivet Discourse are not isolated incidents but the culmination of a trajectory of conflict between Jesus and "this generation." The conflict is about future judgment from Jesus' point of view even though the year 70 is past from our perspective. From Jesus' side, the destruction of Jerusalem was the culmination of the conflict he was experiencing with the Jewish religious leaders. From their side, the conflict would end in Jesus' defeat in crucifixion. Jesus was fully aware of this outcome and of his subsequent resurrection.[8]

This overview of the growing conflict between Jesus and the current Jewish religious and political leadership is important for several reasons. First, we so quickly read the Gospels with an eye toward applying them to our current situation in the twenty-first century that we often miss how they are historically rooted in Jesus' life and ministry. Jesus stood in

---

8. Mark 8:31; 9:9, 12, 31; 10:34, 45; 14:21, 41.

conflict with the reigning religious establishment for the hearts and minds of the nation. The current generation by and large followed the religious leaders in their rejection of Jesus. Jesus knew that by rejecting him they were setting themselves on a course of action that could only lead, by way of false messianic claimants, to war with Rome and utter destruction. Jesus was proclaiming a different kind of kingdom, a kingdom without borders or armies. He was rejected, and the nation marched forward toward inevitable destruction.

Second, awareness of this historical context allows us to see more accurately how the Olivet Discourse does concern the future from Jesus' perspective; it frees us from the notion that Jesus ignored the disciples' question about the timing of the destruction of the temple to give them an answer about events that would transpire thousands of years later. Jesus' focus on the destruction of Jerusalem in the Olivet Discourse in the imminent future represents the culmination of the conflict with the Jewish leadership, which had been growing throughout his ministry.

Truth Touches Life: Our Generation

Our discussion so far in this chapter has focused on the original historical context of Jesus and his generation, but it's also important to consider how this might apply to us and our current generation. The Gospels are written for us today as well—they're written for our instruction (2 Tim. 3:16–17). We've seen Jesus' struggle with the religious and political leaders of his day and how their stubborn and unrepentant hearts ultimately led to the fall of the whole nation.

Turning to ourselves, we can ask, "What about *our* generation?" This question is particularly relevant for leaders, but every Christian has a sphere of influence. Are we staying faithful to God's Word? Are we preaching and confronting this generation with her sin and warning of future judgment? Do we seek to find out what breaks our Lord's heart? Do we mourn for the injustices and the immoral ways of *this* generation?

In the same way that the religious leaders of Jesus' day were preoccupied with the status quo of political and religious correctness and thus blind to the fact that the Messiah had visited them, we can easily become blind to what God is seeking to accomplish in advancing his kingdom in the world today. Join us in prayer that God's appointed leaders in the spiritual realm will stand up and lead God's people with both faithful teaching and holy living in this generation!

Chapter 7

A Call to Patient Waiting for the Coming of the Son of Man

Awareness of the conflict between Jesus and the leaders of that current generation helps us see the importance and relevance of Jesus' message about the destruction of the temple. As we sought to show in Part 1, however, Jesus goes beyond the events of the year 70 in the Olivet Discourse to discuss his future coming as well. He answers the disciples' question about when the temple would be destroyed but he also addresses their question about his coming and the end of the age.

Many readers interested in what Jesus taught about the future are primarily interested in what he taught about his second coming and the end of the age. So far in Part 2, we have focused on what Jesus predicted about the immediate future: (1) his followers would be persecuted; and (2) Jerusalem would be destroyed in judgment as the culmination of the nation's rejection of Jesus. Jesus' comments about persecution were immediately relevant and still relate to us today while his comments about the destruction of Jerusalem were fulfilled in the year 70. We are now at a point where we can explore what Jesus taught about his second coming and the end of the present evil age of sin and oppression.

Jesus identified himself as the Son of Man prophesied in Daniel 7:13–14 and by doing so also claimed that he would come to receive "dominion and glory and a kingdom, that all peoples, nations, and languages should serve him" (Dan. 7:14). In this chapter, we'll consider Jesus' teaching about the coming of the Son of Man. It will become evident that Daniel 7:13 was likely used by Jesus to refer to two events: his "coming" to the Father in the immediate future to be enthroned at God's right hand and his coming in the distant future to fully establish his kingdom on earth. We'll also consider Jesus' teaching about the need for patient waiting and the unspecified period of time that would need to elapse between these two comings.

The Son of Man

One of the most characteristic designations of Jesus in all four Gospels is the title "Son of Man." Jesus often spoke of himself as the Son of Man when discussing his earthly ministry, his imminent suffering, and his future coming in glory. Some interpreters argue that "son of man" means little more than "human being" or "I" (it does mean this in a few passages) but there is growing acceptance of the fact that "son of man" did have pre-Christian Jewish messianic connotations and Jesus' use of it was likely linked with Daniel 7:13 by some of his first hearers.[*]

Blomberg helpfully notes that "'Son of Man' winds up being a very exalted title for Jesus. *It does not primarily focus on his true humanity but on his heavenly enthronement. . . .* It is more of a synonym than an antonym of 'Son of God.' But it remains ambiguous enough that Jesus was able to invest the term with his own meaning and clarifications. It was not susceptible to the political misunderstandings surrounding the term 'Messiah' itself."[**] Jesus thus used the term because it would indicate his close connection to God in the fulfillment of God's purposes without carrying the socio-political baggage of a more explicitly messianic title.

---

[*] See the extensive use of "son of man" in 1 Enoch 37–41. Even though this section of 1 Enoch cannot be dated with certainty, it likely reflects at least some pre-Christian ideas. For further discussion see Michael B. Shepherd, "Daniel 7:13 and the New Testament Son of Man," *WTJ* 68 (2006): 99–111; Karl A. Kuhn, "The 'One like a Son of Man' Becomes the 'Son of God,'" *CBQ* 69 *(2007):* 22–42.

[**] Craig L. Blomberg, *Jesus and the Gospels: An Introduction and Survey,* 2nd ed. (Nashville: B & H Academic, 2009), 472–73 (emphasis original).

Matthew: The Coming of the Son of Man

Matthew 10:23

23 When they persecute you in one town, flee to the next, for truly,
I say to you, you will not have gone through all the towns of Israel
before *the Son of Man comes.*

We discussed this passage earlier in chapter 5 regarding future persecution and noted that Jesus is either referring to his enthronement at
God's right hand, which took place at his ascension, or to his final coming to earth in the more distant future. If the latter, Jesus' reference to the
disciples' work in all the towns of Israel is a figurative way of describing
the proclamation of the gospel to the Jewish people throughout history.
In support of this idea is the fact that persecution certainly didn't stop
with Jesus' enthronement at God's right hand. However, we suggested
above that it is more likely that this reference to the coming Son of Man
was fulfilled with Jesus' enthronement and thus represents the already
fulfilled aspect of Jesus' rule when he came to the Father in heaven to
receive his kingdom. This kingdom, however, is a spiritual reality; it has
not yet been physically consummated and is actively opposed on earth at
the present.

Matthew 16:27–17:2

27 For the *Son of Man is going to come* with his angels in the glory of
his Father, and then he will repay each person according to what
he has done. 28 Truly, I say to you, there are some standing here
who will not taste death until they see *the Son of Man coming* in
his kingdom." 1 And after six days Jesus took with him Peter and
James, and John his brother, and led them up a high mountain
by themselves. 2 And he was transfigured before them and his face
shone like the sun, and his clothes became white as light.

This is a very important passage because it brings together both the
"already" and the "not yet" of the coming of the Son of Man. First, Jesus
focuses on the distant future, the "not yet" coming of the Son of Man
with his angels and the glory of his Father. This future coming is closely
associated with the final judgment, which will result in condemnation for

those who have rejected the Son and reward for those who have followed the Son.

Second, however, Jesus notes that "there are some standing here who will not taste death until they see the Son of Man coming in his kingdom." This verse would initially seem to indicate that Jesus thought his glorious future coming would take place during the lifetime of his contemporaries but Matthew, Mark, and Luke all follow these words with the Transfiguration account. This indicates that Jesus' first hearers, the eyewitnesses responsible for the material found in the four Gospels, interpreted Jesus' words about some living who would see the coming of the Son of Man as fulfilled in the Transfiguration.

In the Transfiguration, Jesus is transformed before Peter, James, and John, and they glimpse his real glory: They see him as the exalted and glorified Son of Man. This could be understood as the reality of his glory that was veiled by his incarnate human body but it is preferable to understand it as a preview of his resurrected glory after being enthroned at God's right hand and after receiving dominion, glory, and a kingdom.

Either way, the earliest Christians understood that this fulfilled Jesus' claim that some of those living at the time would see the Son of Man coming in glory: They would see the luminescent appearance of the Lord in advance of his future coming to bring final salvation and judgment with his angels in the glory of his Father.

This initial vision would have inspired his disciples with confidence for the difficult days that lay ahead when it would appear, for a time, as if Jesus was not Daniel's Son of Man and not destined to reign. During Jesus' crucifixion, it certainly wouldn't have appeared to the disciples that Jesus was going to come with any sort of kingdom. Some, however, had glimpsed it in advance; they had briefly seen the glorious Son of Man as he would be following his resurrection, exaltation, and reception of his kingdom.

Matthew 25:31–32

[31] When the *Son of Man comes* in his glory, and all the angels with him, then he will sit on his glorious throne. [32] Before him will be gathered all the nations, and he will separate people one from another as a shepherd separates the sheep from the goats.

This description of the coming of the Son of Man seems to relate to the more distant future coming because it is associated with glory, the activity of the angels, sitting on a glorious throne, and the judgment of "all the nations."

Matthew 26:63–66

> [63] But Jesus remained silent. And the high priest said to him, "I adjure you by the living God, tell us if you are the Christ, the Son of God." [64] Jesus said to him, "You have said so. But I tell you, *from now on* you will see the *Son of Man* seated at the right hand of Power and *coming* on the clouds of heaven." [65] Then the high priest tore his robes and said, "He has uttered blasphemy. What further witnesses do we need? You have now heard his blasphemy. [66] What is your judgment?" They answered, "He deserves death."

Jesus' final reference to the coming of the Son of Man occurs during the Jewish stage of his trial and led to the death sentence on the charge of blasphemy. It's still possible that up to this point Jesus could have avoided death but once he clearly, directly, and publicly identified himself with the individual who would be enthroned at God's right hand as in Psalm 110:1 and the coming Son of Man of Daniel 7:13, his doom was sealed. There was no turning back after that. Jesus' use of the phrase "from now on" and his drawing a connection between Psalm 110:1 and Daniel 7:13 indicates that this "coming of the Son of Man" was fulfilled with Jesus' coming to the Father and subsequent enthronement at God's right hand in heaven.

Matthew: Parables Indicating the Passing of an Unspecific Period Preceding Jesus' Return

Does Jesus give any indication as to how much time might pass before his coming with glory to fully establish his kingdom on earth? We noted in the last chapter how Jesus professed ignorance regarding that future day: "But concerning that day and hour no one knows, not even the angels of heaven, nor the Son, but the Father only" (Matt. 24:36). The earliest Christians shared a fervent hope that Jesus would come soon, but Jesus spent many of his parables preparing them for the necessity of an unspecified—but longer rather than shorter—period preceding his return and the need for patient waiting for his second coming. This is an overt focus of three of the parables directly following the Olivet Discourse.

In chapter 4, we noted the parable at the end of Matthew 24 in which the wait for the master's return was so long that the head servant was in danger of abandoning his duties and abusing his fellow servants (Matt. 24:48–49). This is immediately followed by the parable of the ten virgins, a parable unique to Matthew (25:1–13). Half of the virgins were prepared for a longer-than-expected wait while the other half were unprepared, expecting the bridegroom to arrive quickly. However, the bridegroom was slow in coming (Matt. 25:5). Those who were unprepared for the lengthy period of patient waiting for the bridegroom's arrival found themselves shut out of the marriage feast when the bridegroom finally arrived.

The parable of the talents immediately follows in which a man entrusts his property to servants before going on a journey (Matt. 25:14–30): "*After a long time* the master of those servants came and settled accounts with them" (Matt. 25:19). These parables strengthen our argument above in chapter 3 that Jesus didn't claim that he would come in glory with cosmic upheaval within a generation but rather that the temple would be destroyed within a generation. Jesus didn't know the day or hour of his future coming but knew it would be a long period of time, and he used the parables to equip and prepare his followers for an unspecified interval during which they would experience persecution and opposition even as they proclaimed Jesus and his kingdom to the world.

Mark

Mark 8:38–9:2

[38] "For whoever is ashamed of me and of my words in this adulterous and sinful generation, of him will the Son of Man also be ashamed when he comes in the glory of his Father with the holy angels." [1] And he said to them, "Truly, I say to you, there are some standing here who will not taste death until they see the kingdom of God after it has come with power." [2] And after six days Jesus took with him Peter and James and John, and led them up a high mountain by themselves. And he was transfigured before them.

We discussed this passage above regarding Matthew's Gospel and suggested that it highlights both the "already" and "not yet" aspects of Jesus' coming. The coming of the Son of Man in the glory of his Father with the holy angels points to his future "not yet" second coming while the earliest Christians explicitly connected Jesus' statement in 9:1 with the events of the Transfiguration during which some of those living at the time received a vision of Jesus as a glorified and exalted figure. This could have been a vision of Jesus as he truly was (veiled in his humanity) as he would be following the ascension and his enthronement at God's right hand or as he will be when he physically returns in the future to establish his kingdom fully and completely on earth. The exact referent is less important than the fact that the narrative itself suggests fulfillment: At the Transfiguration, some of Jesus' disciples saw Jesus glorified—the kingdom having come in power.

This is directly parallel to the kingdom itself which is a current reality under Jesus' kingship. Through the direction of the Holy Spirit, the kingdom is already present and expanding in the world today amid intense opposition. The kingdom won't always be opposed, however, and when Jesus physically returns, he'll establish his eternal kingdom. Everyone will see, and every knee will bow. At the Transfiguration, the disciples saw a vision of the exalted King of the coming kingdom as a visionary glimpse, as it were, of the future establishment of Jesus' kingdom on earth.

Mark 14:62

> 62 And Jesus said, "I am, and you will see the Son of Man seated at the right hand of Power, and coming with the clouds of heaven."

At his trial, Jesus is asked if he in fact is the Christ, the Son of the Blessed One, and he replies affirmatively, "I am." He goes further to make a promise that people will see the Son of Man seated at the right hand of power and coming with the clouds of heaven (combining Ps. 110:1 and Dan. 7:13). In Matthew's account, Jesus says, "From now on you will see," a likely indication that Jesus was using Psalm 110:1 and Daniel 7:13 to refer to his forthcoming ascension and enthronement at God's right hand (Matt. 26:64). Mark doesn't include this temporal indicator, so it is less clear whether his words should be understood as referring to Jesus' immediate future ascension and enthronement or his more distant second coming. Following Matthew's lead, it is better to read Jesus' words at his trial in Mark as indicating his ascension and enthronement at God's right hand, which would take place soon after his crucifixion and resurrection.

Luke

Luke's version of Jesus' words at the trial seems to confirm this point. In Luke, Jesus states, "But from now on the Son of Man shall be seated at the right hand of the power of God" (Luke 22:69). Unlike Matthew and Mark who both use the language of the coming Son of Man drawn from Daniel 7:13 to refer to two distinct events (either the near future ascension and enthronement or the distant future second coming), Luke seems to reserve this language exclusively for Jesus' second coming. In Matthew and Luke, the context is necessary to determine whether Daniel 7:13 is being used to refer to Jesus' ascension and enthronement at God's right hand in the imminent future or his second coming.

Luke's preference for using Daniel 7:13 solely to refer to Jesus' second coming is evident from Jesus' trial. As noted in the prior section, in Matthew and Mark, Jesus boldly claims to be both the enthroned individual of Psalm 110:1 and the coming Son of Man of Daniel 7:13. Matthew indicates that these verses are being used to refer to Jesus' imminent ascension and enthronement by adding the phrase "from now on" (Matt. 26:64). Luke maintains this immediate referent ("from now on") but omits Daniel 7:13 from Jesus' answer, so that in Luke Jesus responds only by claiming to be the one who will be enthroned at God's right hand from Psalm 110:1.

It is very likely that by the time Luke wrote his Gospel, Christians were widely connecting Jesus' use of Daniel 7:13 with his second coming, so Luke may have omitted Jesus' reference to the passage to avoid confusion and to make clear that at his trial Jesus was referring to his enthronement at God's right hand as prophesied by Psalm 110:1 and not his second coming. Luke recognized the confusion that could be caused by applying Daniel 7:13 to two events separated by a long period. This means that when Luke does refer to Daniel 7:13, we should understand this as a reference to Jesus' second coming from his position at God's right hand to establish his kingdom on earth. This consistent usage is demonstrated by the texts themselves.

Luke 9:26–29

> [26] For whoever is ashamed of me and of my words, of him will the Son of Man be ashamed when he comes in his glory and the glory of the Father and of the holy angels. [27] But I tell you truly, there are some standing here who will not taste death until they see the kingdom of God." [28] Now about eight days after these sayings he took with him Peter and John and James and went up on the mountain to pray. [29] And as he was praying, the appearance of his face was altered, and his clothing became dazzling white.

We've discussed this passage in Matthew and Mark and don't need to spend much time on it here. The coming of the Son of Man in verse 26 is associated with judgment, the glory of the Father, and the angels. This is a clear reference to Jesus' second coming. Verse 27, on the other hand, refers in Luke to the imminent inauguration of the kingdom of God. As with Matthew and Mark, the narrative arrangement of the Transfiguration account following this pronouncement indicates that the Transfiguration plays some role in fulfilling Jesus' words through providing a vision of the exalted and glorified King. Also, Luke, more so than other Gospel authors, focuses on the "already" aspect of the inauguration of the kingdom, so it is very natural to read verse 27 in Luke's account as the inauguration of God's kingdom, which would commence with Jesus' ascension and enthronement at God's right hand.

Luke 12:35–48

> "Stay dressed for action and keep your lamps burning, [36] and be like men who are waiting for their master to come home from the wedding feast, so that they may open the door to him at once when he comes and knocks. [37] Blessed are those servants whom the master finds awake when he comes. Truly, I say to you, he will dress himself for service and have them recline at table, and he will come and serve them. [38] If he comes in the second watch, or in the third, and finds them awake, blessed are those servants!
> [39] But know this, that if the master of the house had known at what hour the thief was coming, he would not have left his house

to be broken into. [40] You also must be ready, for *the Son of Man is coming* at an hour you do not expect."

[41] Peter said, "Lord, are you telling this parable for us or for all?" [42] And the Lord said, "Who then is the faithful and wise manager, whom his master will set over his household, to give them their portion of food at the proper time? [43] Blessed is that servant whom his master will find so doing when he comes. [44] Truly, I say to you, he will set him over all his possessions. [45] But if that servant says to himself, '*My master is delayed* in coming,' and begins to beat the male and female servants, and to eat and drink and get drunk, [46] the master of that servant will come on a day when he does not expect him and at an hour he does not know, and will cut him in pieces and put him with the unfaithful. [47] And that servant who knew his master's will but did not get ready or act according to his will, will receive a severe beating. [48] But the one who did not know, and did what deserved a beating, will receive a light beating. Everyone to whom much was given, of him much will be required, and from him to whom they entrusted much, they will demand the more."

Luke here gathers three short parables related to the future coming of the Son of Man. The first parable is also found at the end of the Olivet Discourse in Mark's account (13:34–36) while the second and third are found at the end of the Olivet Discourse in Matthew (24:42–51). The location is different in Luke but the main point of each parable is similar; they stress the unexpected nature of Jesus' return, the reality of a lengthy, unspecific period preceding the second coming, and the need to remain vigilant and active in our duties even though the master is physically absent. The master's return will be a time of punishment for those who were negligent in their duties and a time of reward for those who were faithful.

Luke 17:20–37

[20] Being asked by the Pharisees when the kingdom of God would come, he answered them, "The kingdom of God is not coming in ways that can be observed, [21] nor will they say, 'Look, here it is!' or 'There!' for behold, the kingdom of God is in the midst of you."

[22] And he said to the disciples, "The days are coming when

you will desire to see one of the days of the Son of Man, and you will not see it. ²³ And they will say to you, 'Look, there!' or 'Look, here!' Do not go out or follow them. ²⁴ For as the lightning flashes and lights up the sky from one side to the other, so will the Son of Man be in his day. ²⁵ But first he must suffer many things and be rejected by this generation. ²⁶ Just as it was in the days of Noah, so will it be in the days of the Son of Man. ²⁷ They were eating and drinking and marrying and being given in marriage, until the day when Noah entered the ark, and the flood came and destroyed them all. ²⁸ Likewise, just as it was in the days of Lot—they were eating and drinking, buying and selling, planting and building, ²⁹ but on the day when Lot went out from Sodom, fire and sulfur rained from heaven and destroyed them all— ³⁰ so will it be on the day when the Son of Man is revealed. ³¹ On that day, let the one who is on the housetop, with his goods in the house, not come down to take them away, and likewise let the one who is in the field not turn back. ³² Remember Lot's wife. ³³ Whoever seeks to preserve his life will lose it, but whoever loses his life will keep it. ³⁴ I tell you, in that night there will be two in one bed. One will be taken and the other left. ³⁵ There will be two women grinding together. One will be taken and the other left."[1] ³⁷ And they said to him, "Where, Lord?" He said to them, "Where the corpse is, there the vultures will gather."

In chapter 4 above, we noted that the extended ending of the Olivet Discourse in Matthew has several parallels with these verses in Luke 17. This could indicate that Jesus spoke these words on a different occasion and Matthew and Luke both placed the teaching at thematically appropriate places in their respective Gospels.

In Luke's Gospel, some of the Pharisees ask Jesus when the kingdom of God would come. Jesus responds rather quickly by making the astounding claim that the kingdom of God was already present in their midst. The kingdom of God had been inaugurated in and through Jesus' life—the King himself was present in their midst!

---

1. Verse 36 is omitted in most ancient manuscripts and modern translations.

Jesus then turns his attention to his disciples and prepares them for the unspecified period of time that will occur between his ascension and second coming. They will long for Jesus to be present, but their longing must not lead them to be deceived by false messiahs. The real coming of the Son of Man will be unmistakable and visible to all, like lightning flashing across the sky. That day will be like the days of Noah and Lot when judgment came suddenly on unbelievers. There will be no warning, and people will be carrying on with life as usual. Most likely, the comparison to the days of Lot and Noah also indicates typologically that evil and wickedness will be particularly intense right before the judgment.

The warning against turning back or trying to gather material possessions makes the same point about unexpectedness—there will be no time to prepare when the Son of Man comes. All preparation must be accomplished in advance through a lifetime of faithful discipleship. As with Matthew, those taken are removed in judgment and the ones saved are left behind. The section closes with Jesus' enigmatic answer to the disciples' question about where this would take place. In Matthew, this proverb about the vultures is closely associated with the example of lightning flashing across the sky; it likely makes the same point here in Luke. Jesus' coming will be visible to all, so it doesn't particularly matter where one is geographically on that day.

Luke 18:8

⁸ "Nevertheless, when the Son of Man comes, will he find faith on earth?"

Jesus presents this question to promote self-refection in his hearers and motivate them to persevere. Jesus will find faith, but the challenges are great and the disciples will need to be prepared through vigilance and persistent prayer.

Parable of Waiting and Conflict (Luke 19:11–27)

Luke shares the parable of the talents/minas with Matthew but his version contains a few unique elements. First, Luke highlights the fact that Jesus told the parable "because they supposed that the kingdom of God was to appear immediately" (19:11). Jesus counters their imminent expectation by telling this parable of a nobleman who went to a far country to receive a kingdom. The trip would take a long time. This closely parallels the way in which Jesus would soon ascend to the Father to receive his kingdom. Second, Luke includes an element of adversity with new characters—citizens. The citizens of the kingdom "hated him and sent a delegation after him, saying, 'We do not want this man to reign over us'" (19:14). This transparently relates to Jesus' rejection by his own people: "When he returned, having received the kingdom," he settled accounts with the three servants and executed those who had opposed his reign (19:15). This parable doesn't use "Son of Man" language but seems to be pointing to Jesus' second coming.

The Annunciation (Luke 1:32–33)

Although this passage doesn't use "Son of Man" terminology, it is worth mentioning. When the angel informed Mary of Jesus' birth, he used the following words: "He will be great and will be called the Son of the Most High. And the Lord God will give to him the throne of his father David, and he will reign over the house of Jacob forever, and of his kingdom there will be no end" (1:32–33). As discussed above, Jesus inaugurated his kingdom over God's people through his life, death, resurrection, ascension, and enthronement. The angel's words, however, seem to point beyond this initial enthronement toward the final and complete establishment of Jesus' eternal kingdom on earth.

Summary: The Coming of the Son of Man

Jesus spoke of the coming of the Son of Man in two distinct ways. Sometimes he referred to his coming to the Father to receive a kingdom; this was fulfilled with his ascension and enthronement at God's right hand. At other times, he described his future glorious coming to earth accompanied by angels. Through parables, Jesus prepared his followers for a long period between his departure and return.

This already/not yet aspect to the coming of the Son of Man resembles the way in which God's kingdom has already been inaugurated through the enthronement of God's Son but not yet been physically consummated on earth. Several of Jesus' references to his coming after an unspecified period of time connect his coming with judgment and salvation. In the following chapter, we'll consider the events that Jesus taught would follow the coming of the Son of Man.

Chapter 8

Future Resurrection, Judgment, Reward, and Punishment

Jesus' second coming is associated with two other distant future events in the Gospels: resurrection and final judgment. Although there are far more references to future judgment than to resurrection in the Gospels, a future resurrection was a central future of the Jewish and early Christian worldview. Resurrection receives less explicit attention because it was an expectation shared by Jesus with most of his contemporaries (excluding the politically powerful Sadducees). The resurrection is closely connected to the final judgment, but we'll discuss these separately as the chapter progresses.

Future Resurrection

Matthew 22:23–33 (cf. Mark 12:18–27; Luke 20:27–40)

[23] The same day Sadducees came to him, who say that there is no resurrection, and they asked him a question, [24] saying, "Teacher, Moses said, 'If a man dies having no children, his brother must marry the widow and raise up offspring for his brother.' [25] Now there were seven brothers among us. The first married and died, and having no offspring left his wife to his brother. [26] So too the second and third, down to the seventh. [27] After them all, the woman died. [28] In the resurrection, therefore, of the seven, whose wife will she be? For they all had her." [29] But Jesus answered them, "You are wrong, because you know neither the Scriptures nor the power of God. [30] For in the resurrection they neither marry nor

are given in marriage, but are like angels in heaven. [31] And as for the resurrection of the dead, have you not read what was said to you by God: [32] 'I am the God of Abraham, and the God of Isaac, and the God of Jacob'? He is not God of the dead, but of the living." [33] And when the crowd heard it, they were astonished at his teaching.

During the same day on which Jesus spoke his conflict parables against the Jewish religious leaders and the Olivet Discourse, some Sadducees attempted to trap him with what they thought was a trick question. The Sadducees started querying him by appealing to Moses, Israel's lawgiver, regarding levirate marriage where the brother of a deceased man has an obligation to marry that man's widow and she has an obligation to marry him.[1] In his response, Jesus critiqued the Sadducees' ignorance of both the Scriptures and the power of God.

The Sadducees' position was clear and well known: "There is no resurrection." Josephus describes them further:

> The Sadducees . . . do away with Fate altogether, and remove God beyond, not merely the commission, but the very sight, of evil. They maintain that man has the free choice of good or evil, and that it rests with each man's will whether he follows the one or the other. As for the persistence of the soul after death, penalties in the underworld, and rewards, they will have none of them. (*Jewish War* 2.164–65)

Jesus responds to their trick question and moves on to present a positive argument for the future resurrection based on an easily overlooked grammatical point. God is—present tense—the God of Abraham, Isaac, and Jacob. This means that Abraham, Isaac, and Jacob must still exist. In Jesus' answer, he doesn't indicate that those resurrected would *be* angels

---

1. The law concerning levirate marriage can be found in Deuteronomy 25:5–6: "If brothers dwell together, and one of them dies and has no son, the wife of the dead man shall not be married outside the family to a stranger. Her husband's brother shall go in to her and take her as his wife and perform the duty of a husband's brother to her. And the first son whom she bears shall succeed to the name of his dead brother, that his name may not be blotted out of Israel."

but rather that they would be *like* angels regarding their lack of procreation. Craig Keener observes,

> Most Jewish people agreed that angels did not eat, drink, or propagate (*1 Enoch* 15:6–7). Some Jewish traditions also compared the righteous after death with angels (*1 Enoch* 39:5; 104:2–4; *2 Baruch* 51:10–11). Since angels did not die (unless God destroyed them), they had no need to procreate. Jesus' statement about lack of marriage and procreation in heaven (Matt. 22:30) follows largely from the logic of the resurrection.[2]

When the crowd heard Jesus' response, they were astonished at his teaching, probably because they had never heard that specific answer before in response to the Sadducees' rejection of a future resurrection.

In Jesus' discussion with the Sadducees, he was responding to them but not particularly trying to win the crowd over to his view. Most people in Israel at the time followed the teaching of the Pharisees and would have already affirmed belief in the future resurrection of the godly.

Truth Touches Life: Hope

Belief in Jesus' resurrection sets Christianity apart from all other major world religions. It's impossible to overstate the importance of Jesus' resurrection for Christianity; without it the earliest believers would have had nothing to proclaim. Jesus' resurrection is also the source of our future home. In 1 Corinthians 15, Paul makes some bold assertions.

First, he makes clear that the truth of Christianity depends upon Jesus' resurrection: "But if there is no resurrection of the dead, then not even Christ has been raised. And if Christ has not been raised, then our preaching is in vain and your faith is in vain" (1 Cor. 15:13–14).

Second, Paul cites the reality of Jesus' past resurrection as

---

2. Craig S. Keener, *Matthew*, IVP New Testament Commentary (Downers Grove, IL: InterVarsity Press, 1997), 328.

the guarantee of our future resurrection. Jesus' resurrection was the firstfruits of the much larger future harvest. His resurrection was the first of many. Our future hope as Christians is in the risen Lord and Savior of humankind, the man Jesus Christ, and it is through his resurrection that we have life right now and are promised life with him in the age to come!

Matthew 8:11–12 (Future Resurrection)

¹¹ I tell you, many will come from east and west and recline at table with Abraham, Isaac, and Jacob in the kingdom of heaven, ¹² while the sons of the kingdom will be thrown into the outer darkness. In that place there will be weeping and gnashing of teeth.

The theme of resurrection doesn't often feature as an individual theme but is frequently assumed as part of a bigger scenario involving future final judgment. This reference to the resurrection is easy to miss but the fact that many will recline with Abraham, Isaac, and Jacob in the future kingdom of heaven surely indicates that Abraham, Isaac, and Jacob will possess resurrected bodies. This passing reference bears witness to the way in which the future resurrection was assumed; unless dialoging with Sadducees (who didn't believe in a bodily resurrection), there was no need to argue for its reality.

These verses also bear witness to the growing conflict between Jesus and his unbelieving Jewish contemporaries. The rightful (ethnic) sons of the kingdom would lose their place and experience judgment because of unbelief, while God's kingdom would be populated by people from around the world.

Other References to Resurrection

Various shorter references indicate that Jesus assumed the reality of the future resurrection of the righteous. In preparation for future persecution, Jesus instructed his disciples not to fear those who can kill only the body (Luke 12:4). These people shouldn't be feared because they can do nothing more than kill the body; they have no power to prevent resurrection. A few chapters later, Jesus encouraged his hearers to take care of the poor, crippled, lame, and blind for the sole reason that they had no means of repayment (Luke 14:13). Instead of monetary repayment, "You will be repaid at the resurrection of the just" (Luke 14:14). The just will experience resurrection to take part in Jesus' eternal kingdom. As mentioned above, the reality of a future resurrection doesn't receive as much explicit attention in the Gospels because apart from the Sadducees it was a common belief shared by Jesus with his Palestinian contemporaries. Jesus doesn't add anything to this doctrine in the Synoptic Gospels (although John records some startling comments about the relationship of the future resurrection to Jesus' own life and ministry).[3]

Matthew: The Final Judgment and Eternal Reward and Punishment

In contrast to the future resurrection, Jesus often spoke about the future judgment that would either lead to eternal condemnation or salvation. Most of Jesus' teaching about the distant future focused on the final judgment, and it is the central element of Jesus' teaching about the end time.

As you study Jesus' teaching about the final judgment in this chapter, it would be worth considering the role of the final judgment in your own thinking. Do you ever think about it? Do you often hear about it at church in preaching and teaching? Although there is the danger of overemphasizing the reality of future judgment, it is also very possible to underestimate its significance and ignore its importance. In view of its importance to Jesus, we neglect the topic to our own peril.

Matthew, more so than Mark, Luke, or John, emphasizes Jesus' warnings of judgment. It's not always immediately evident whether the focus of judgment is on the year 70 or the final judgment of all humanity, but often the context will provide clues.

Matthew 3:12

12 His winnowing fork is in his hand, and he will clear his threshing floor and gather his wheat into the barn, but the chaff he will burn with unquenchable fire.

---

3. See chapter 9 below.

Before Jesus came onto the scene, John the Baptist served as his fore-runner. Jesus' preaching mirrored that of John in several ways. They both proclaimed the coming of God's kingdom and urged repentance.[4] They also both focused on the reality of future judgment to motivate people to repent. This statement by John is directed toward Jesus. He is the one with the winnowing fork in his hand who is about to examine his people. This winnowing activity is an unmistakable reference to judgment:

> At harvest time the grain was threshed, for example, by having oxen tread it out, a process that shook the grain free from the husks but left them in the same heap. It was then winnowed: the threshed grain was separated from the husks by throwing it into the air, at first with a fork and later with a shovel (cf. Isa. 30:24). The heavier grain would fall straight down, but the lighter husks would be blown further away.[5]

The fact that the winnowing folk is already in Jesus' hand signifies that separation is about to begin. This separation is the last step before judgment in the form of unquenchable fire. John is here focusing on the imminence of judgment. Chaff signifies the wicked in general, and in this context the Pharisees and Sadducees who stand opposed to John's baptism. Wheat is a reference to those who respond to John's message with repentance in preparation for the kingdom of heaven.[6] This reference to judgment could be viewed as fulfilled in the events of the year 70 but, if so, they are typologically pointing forward to the final judgment.

Matthew 7:19–23

[19] Every tree that does not bear good fruit is cut down and thrown into the fire. [20] Thus you will recognize them by their fruits. [21] Not everyone who says to me, "Lord, Lord," will enter the kingdom of heaven, but the one who does the will of my Father who is in heaven. [22] On *that day* many will say to me, "Lord, Lord, did we

---

4. "Repent, for the kingdom of heaven is at hand" (Matt. 3:2; cf. Jesus in Matt. 4:17).

5. Leon Morris, *The Gospel according to Matthew*, PNTC (Grand Rapids: Eerdmans, 1992), 62.

6. Warren Carter, *Matthew and the Margins: A Sociopolitical and Religious Reading* (Sheffield: Sheffield Academic Press, 2000), 100.

not prophesy in your name, and cast out demons in your name, and do many mighty works in your name?" [23] And then will I declare to them, "I never knew you; depart from me, you workers of lawlessness."

In this section of the Sermon on the Mount, Jesus is warning people to beware of false prophets. How are they to recognize them? By their fruits: For a good tree cannot bear bad fruit and vice versa (Matt. 7:15–18). Jesus then speaks of the impending judgment on these false prophets. The language "'is cut down and cast into the fire,' is the common metaphorical language of eschatological judgment already encountered in Matthew 3:10, 12 (cf. 13:40, 42, 50; 18:8–9; 25:41; Luke 13:6–9; John 15:6)."[7] Judgment is often associated with fire and burning.

At least two powerful points surface from this section. First, Jesus presents himself as the judge in that final day. People will appeal to him and he'll respond to them. Jesus' verdict will determine their destiny. This is a claim no ordinary human being could make; it was widely known that God himself would be the judge on that final day, and Jesus' claim here closely associates himself with this divine activity.

Second, entrance into God's kingdom doesn't depend on prophecy, casting out demons, or performing miracles; it hinges entirely on doing God's will. This functions as a warning which is intended to shock hearers into a soul-searching response. It doesn't matter what wonderful things you and I have accomplished in our lives if we fail to do God's will. It's quite possible that many people are deceived with false assurance of a secure relationship with God when their actions demonstrate that they're not living in a vital life-giving relationship with Jesus. The day will come when they will want to enter the kingdom of heaven based on their human accomplishments but Jesus will reply, "I never knew you; depart from me, you workers of lawlessness." Outward appearances and impressions don't always make for a repentant and contrite heart nor do impressive achievements make for true fellowship with the Son. Therefore, it's likely that Jesus is here referring to the final day of judgment and the establishment of God's kingdom.

---

7. Hagner, *Matthew 1–13*, 184.

Matthew 8:11–12 (Final Judgment)

> ¹¹ I tell you, many will come from east and west and recline at table with Abraham, Isaac, and Jacob in the kingdom of heaven, ¹² while the sons of the kingdom will be thrown into the outer darkness. In that place there will be weeping and gnashing of teeth.

Leading up to these words, a Gentile centurion had just amazed Jesus with faith unequaled in all of Israel. Jesus' response highlights how people like the centurion will come into God's kingdom from around the world while the presumed citizens of the kingdom will be excluded in judgment. Earlier in this chapter, we mentioned that in Matthew's Gospel the theme of resurrection is generally associated with the theme of judgment. In Matthew 22:23–33, Jesus educates the Sadducees regarding the fact that God is not the God of the dead but of the living. Here Jesus talks about a time when people will dine with the patriarchs in the kingdom of heaven, a statement that presupposes the reality of the resurrection.

Jesus' discussion of the future judgment focuses on two potential outcomes: entrance into the kingdom or exclusion from the kingdom in outer darkness. This outer darkness is further described with the vivid imagery of weeping and gnashing of teeth and likely refers to the future final judgment and not just the events of the year 70.

Matthew 12:41–42

> ⁴¹ The men of Nineveh will rise up at the judgment with this generation and condemn it, for they repented at the preaching of Jonah, and behold, something greater than Jonah is here. ⁴² The queen of the South will rise up at the judgment with this generation and condemn it, for she came from the ends of the earth to hear the wisdom of Solomon, and behold, something greater than Solomon is here.

This verse could be understood as indicating the general resurrection with the presence of the people of Nineveh and the queen of the South at the final judgment, but it is not clear that Jesus' words were meant to make that point. The focus on "this generation" highlights Jesus' contemporaries, but the saying seems to indicate the verdict passed against the current generation at the final judgment and not just the destructive judgment of the year 70.

Matthew 13:36–43 (The Parable of the Weeds)

³⁶ Then he left the crowds and went into the house. And his disciples came to him, saying, "Explain to us the parable of the weeds of the field." ³⁷ He answered, "The one who sows the good seed is the Son of Man. ³⁸ The field is the world, and the good seed is the sons of the kingdom. The weeds are the sons of the evil one, ³⁹ and the enemy who sowed them is the devil. The harvest is the end of the age, and the reapers are angels. ⁴⁰ Just as the weeds are gathered and burned with fire, so will it be at the end of the age. ⁴¹ The Son of Man will send his angels, and they will gather out of his kingdom all causes of sin and all law-breakers, ⁴² and throw them into the fiery furnace. In that place there will be weeping and gnashing of teeth. ⁴³ Then the righteous will shine like the sun in the kingdom of their Father. He who has ears, let him hear."

At the end of the age, the "sons of the evil one" will be removed from the kingdom and "burned with fire" in the "fiery furnace" while the "sons of the kingdom" will be privileged to experience life in the Father's kingdom. The coming of the Son of Man here refers to his final coming because it is associated with the end of the age and final salvation and judgment. The scenario entails the Son of Man sending his angels to remove sinners and every cause of sin. This is parallel to how Jesus warned people of the coming judgment at the end of Matthew's version of the Olivet Discourse: In that day, one will be taken away in judgment while one will be left (Matt. 24:40–41). We want to be among those who are left behind and privileged to "shine like the sun in the kingdom of the Father."

Matthew 13:47–50 (The Parable of the Dragnet)

⁴⁷ Again, the kingdom of heaven is like a net that was thrown into the sea and gathered fish of every kind. ⁴⁸ When it was full, men drew it ashore and sat down and sorted the good into containers but threw away the bad. ⁴⁹ So it will be at the end of the age. The angels will come out and separate the evil from the righteous

⁵⁰ and throw them into the fiery furnace. In that place there will be weeping and gnashing of teeth.

This kingdom parable follows closely after the parable of the weeds and likewise focuses on judgment. This time Jesus compares the kingdom to a net thrown into the sea that gathered all kinds of fish. The focus of the parable is not on the present state of the church but on the sifting that would take place at the final judgment. The angels who have already been described as servants of the harvest will come to separate the evil from the righteous even as fishermen separate bad fish from the good. As in the parable of the weeds, this parable indicates that the evil will be thrown into a fiery furnace with weeping and gnashing of teeth. As elsewhere, "weeping and gnashing of teeth" signifies utter pain and distress.

Matthew 18:9

⁹ And if your eye causes you to sin, tear it out and throw it away. It is better for you to enter life with one eye than with two eyes to be thrown into the hell of fire.

Jesus here uses hyperbole to emphasize the need for radical self-discipline and sacrifice in the struggle against sin. Because sin is so serious, Jesus discusses stringent measures one ought to take to combat it. It's evident that Jesus is using rhetorical hyperbole; he doesn't intend for his followers literally to maim themselves. Rather, his main point is that believers must resist sin at all costs. Jesus here presents sin as our personal responsibility. It's not up to someone else to fix us and there's no benefit in blaming others. Jesus' brief saying also indicates that the future hell of fire is real. Jesus uses the reality and horror of this future judgment to motivate hearers to respond with repentance and action. Sin must be avoided at all costs!

Matthew 19:27–29

²⁷ Then Peter said in reply, "See, we have left everything and followed you. What then will we have?" ²⁸ Jesus said to them, "Truly, I say to you, in the new world, when the Son of Man will sit on his glorious throne, you who have followed me will also sit on twelve thrones, judging the twelve tribes of Israel. ²⁹ And everyone who has left houses or brothers or sisters or father or mother or

children or lands, for my name's sake, will receive a hundred-fold and will inherit eternal life.

This is a fascinating passage. Jesus isn't primarily trying to teach about the future but is discussing the topics of wealth and rewards. His disciples had left behind everything to follow him and needed assurance that all their sacrifice would be worth it in the end. Jesus assures them that they would be richly recompensed and inherit eternal life. The number is figurative and doesn't point to a literal hundredfold increase. (How would one get one hundred fathers and mothers unless this is figuratively pointing to the abundance of spiritual fathers and mothers in the community of faith?) The mention of eternal life points forward to the result of the final judgment for God's people. They'll have nothing to fear and will instead receive the essence of God's promises, eternal life. Jesus is describing his enthronement "in the new world" (literally, "at the renewal or regeneration"); this points to his second coming and the full physical establishment of his kingdom.

Most uniquely, in this passage Jesus indicates that his disciples will share his rule in some measure, judging the twelve tribes of Israel. This statement needs some further discussion. What does it mean to judge? As France observes,

> If the term carries the sense of an appointed ruler as in the OT "judges" who led Israel before the time of Samuel, the disciples may be understood as the leading representatives of the community to which they themselves belong. But if it carries its more normal sense of judicial decision, the disciples (though themselves Jewish) are set over against Israel, with authority to pronounce judgment on it.[8]

It's difficult to decide between these two options, and even though we're primarily focusing on Matthew in this chapter, it'll be helpful to explore how some of the earliest Christians interpreted Jesus' words. Luke contains a similar statement at the last supper: "You are those who have stayed with me in my trials, and I assign to you, as my Father assigned to me, a

---

8. France, *Gospel of Matthew*, 744.

kingdom, that you may eat and drink at my table in my kingdom and sit on thrones judging the twelve tribes of Israel" (Luke 22:28–30).

In his first letter to the Corinthians, Paul makes a comment, almost in passing, which either reflects a common tradition or explicitly builds on these sayings of Jesus: "Or do you not know that believers will judge the world?" (1 Cor. 6:2). Here Paul has likely expanded and applied Jesus' statement. The original disciples are representative of all God's people, and the twelve tribes of Israel are representative of the whole world. In Revelation 3:21, all who overcome are promised the right to sit with Jesus on his throne. The millennial vision of Revelation 20:4–6 may also relate to Jesus' words, though there is no mention of the twelve apostles or the people of Israel. John's vision of the millennium shares with Paul the expansion of Jesus' words to include all faithful believers and the entire world. John's last vision ends with the phrase "and they will reign forever and ever" (Rev. 22:5). This describes the activity of believers in the eternal kingdom as an exercise of rule over God's creation in fulfillment of his original intention for humanity at creation (Gen. 1:26–28).

Returning to Jesus' words, it would be safe to follow the lead of Paul and John and view the disciples as representatives of all believers and the twelve tribes of Israel as representatives of the entire world. This is not as different from Jesus' intent as might at first appear. It is evident that the twelve thrones shouldn't automatically be linked to the original twelve disciples because Judas disqualified himself and was replaced by Matthias. There is a symbolic meaning to the number twelve. Why did Jesus not call seven, ten, or thirteen disciples? He intentionally called twelve to make a significant point about how he was inaugurating the renewal of Israel. Jesus was reconstituting and renewing the Old Testament people of God, but instead of ethnicity he put himself forward as the determining factor for who would be included or excluded. Jesus presents allegiance to himself as the necessary requirement: Ethnic Jews who rejected Jesus lost their place in Jesus' renewed Israel while non-Jews who embraced him through faith were included.[9] The fact that the twelve disciples—representing renewed

---

9. John, in fact, makes a similar point when he records Jesus as saying, "Behold, I will make those of the synagogue of Satan who say that they are Jews and are not, but lie—behold, I will make them come and bow down before your feet, and they will learn that I have loved you" (Rev. 3:9). According to John, Jews who rejected and opposed Jesus and his people lost the right to call themselves Jews, while both Jew and Gentile who

Israel—would function at the end time in a judging relationship toward those who rejected Jesus makes sense of Jesus' words and paves the way for the development we see in Paul and John.

If Paul and John aren't followed in their expansion and application of Jesus' saying, it would be safe to argue that at "the consummation the Twelve will judge the nation of Israel, presumably for its general rejection of Jesus Messiah."[10] This conclusion falls far short of what some interpreters read into the passage. It says nothing of a rapture, a seven-year tribulation, or a thousand-year period; at most, it affirms that the original disciples, as representatives of a renewed Israel, will participate with Jesus in some way in judging the Jewish nation following Jesus' return for its rejection of Jesus.

Matthew 25:31–46

³¹ When the Son of Man comes in his glory, and all the angels with him, then he will sit on his glorious throne. ³² Before him will be gathered all the nations, and he will separate people one from another as a shepherd separates the sheep from the goats. ³³ And he will place the sheep on his right, but the goats on the left. ³⁴ Then the King will say to those on his right, "Come, you who are blessed by my Father, inherit the kingdom prepared for you from the foundation of the world. ³⁵ For I was hungry and you gave me food, I was thirsty and you gave me drink, I was a stranger and you welcomed me, ³⁶ I was naked and you clothed me, I was sick and you visited me, I was in prison and you came to me." ³⁷ Then the righteous will answer him, saying, "Lord, when did we see you hungry and feed you, or thirsty and give you drink? ³⁸ And when did we see you a stranger and welcome you, or naked and clothe you? ³⁹ And when did we see you sick or in prison and visit you?" ⁴⁰ And the King will answer them, "Truly, I say to you, as you did it to one of the least of these my brothers, you did it to me."

⁴¹ Then he will say to those on his left, "Depart from me,

---

embraced Jesus constitute God's renewed people. Inclusion in this new people is based on allegiance to Jesus rather than ethnicity.

10. Carson, "Matthew," 481.

you cursed, into the eternal fire prepared for the devil and his angels. ⁴²For I was hungry and you gave me no food, I was thirsty and you gave me no drink, ⁴³I was a stranger and you did not welcome me, naked and you did not clothe me, sick and in prison and you did not visit me." ⁴⁴Then they also will answer, saying, "Lord, when did we see you hungry or thirsty or a stranger or naked or sick or in prison, and did not minister to you?" ⁴⁵Then he will answer them, saying, "Truly, I say to you, as you did not do it to one of the least of these, you did not do it to me." ⁴⁶And these will go away into eternal punishment, but the righteous into eternal life.

This parabolic block of teaching forms the formal conclusion to the Olivet Discourse in Matthew and fittingly and climactically describes the coming of the Son of Man at the end of the age. The Son of Man will come in glory with his angels to judge all the nations. "All the nations" likely implies a general resurrection, though this isn't explicitly stated. The people of the world are separated based upon their care and concern for those in need: the hungry, thirsty, naked, sick, and imprisoned. Those who have done God's will in caring for the needy are the righteous who will enter with Jesus into the eternal life of the kingdom prepared from the foundation of the world, while all others will be led away into eternal punishment in the eternal fire prepared for the devil and his angels.

This passage is significant because it concludes Matthew's version of the Olivet Discourse with a reference to Jesus' future coming as the Son of Man to bring final salvation and judgment. The preceding parables indicating an unspecified period of time preceding Jesus' second coming must not cause us to miss the fact that Jesus will in fact come again. He won't put off his return indefinitely.

Mark: The Final Judgment and Eternal Reward and Punishment

Mark 8:38

³⁸"For whoever is ashamed of me and of my words in this adulterous and sinful generation, of him will the Son of Man also be ashamed when he comes in the glory of his Father with the holy angels."

We've had occasion to discuss this verse now at several points, but important to note here is the reference to judgment. When Jesus returns, he'll be ashamed of those who were ashamed of him. It implicitly indicates Jesus' active rule in judgment following his return.

Mark 9:43–48

> [43] And if your hand causes you to sin, cut it off. It is better for you to enter life crippled than with two hands to go to hell, to the unquenchable fire. . . . [45] And if your foot causes you to sin, cut it off. It is better for you to enter life lame than with two feet to be thrown into hell. . . . [47] And if your eye causes you to sin, tear it out. It is better for you to enter the kingdom of God with one eye than with two eyes to be thrown into hell, [48] "where their worm does not die and the fire is not quenched."

As we saw in our discussion of Matthew, Jesus here discusses the extreme measures one must go through to fight sin. Jesus directly associates sin with the punishment of hell. The terror and misery of hell is so serious that it must be avoided at all costs. Jesus isn't threatening his hearers but rather warning them of the reality of future punishment for sin. Jesus' description uses the common imagery of fire as the agent of judgment and destruction:

> The metaphor of amputation could hardly be more shocking; this is a matter of ultimate seriousness. Nothing less than eternal life or death is at stake. Christians who disparage "hell-fire preaching" must face the awkward fact that Mark's Jesus (and still more Matthew's and Luke's) envisaged an ultimate separation between life and Gehenna which demanded the most drastic renunciation in order to avoid the unquenchable fire, and that he did not regard even his disciples as immune from the need to examine themselves and take appropriate action.[11]

Mark 10:28–31

> [28] Peter began to say to him, "See, we have left everything and followed you." [29] Jesus said, "Truly, I say to you, there is no one who

---

11. France, *Gospel of Mark*, 383.

has left house or brothers or sisters or mother or father or children or lands, for my sake and for the gospel, [30] who will not receive a hundredfold now in this time, houses and brothers and sisters and mothers and children and lands, with persecutions, and in the age to come eternal life. [31] But many who are first will be last, and the last first."

We discussed this passage above in relation to future persecution, but now it is important to notice Jesus' reference to "eternal life" in the "age to come." The theme of future reward isn't as prominent in the Gospels because it wasn't a point of disagreement between Jesus and his contemporaries. Jesus here affirms a belief that was widely held. This current evil age wouldn't last forever, but Yahweh (God) would come, bring an end to this evil age, and usher in the new coming age. Jesus affirmed this belief with some adjustments. Inclusion or exclusion in the eternal life of that future age wouldn't depend on ethnicity but on how people responded to him and his message. This is an incredibly bold claim and was central to the proclamation of the earliest Christians: "And there is salvation in no one else, for there is no other name under heaven given among men by which we must be saved" (Acts 4:12).

Truth Touches Life: God's Love and Holiness

Jesus taught a lot about a future judgment. Many preachers today have resorted to a very simplistic message that talks almost exclusively about God's love. There's nothing wrong with proclaiming and celebrating God's love; after all, it is the reason why God sent his Son to die on our behalf (John 3:16–17). A problem arises, however, when God's love is emphasized to the exclusion of his holiness. God is love, but he is also holy; therefore, we ought to be preaching God's love *and* his holiness. Of all the attributes of God, people tend to feel most comfortable with love because they feel like it lets them off the hook regarding sin. But God's attributes are a unity; they're not in conflict with each other. It's unhealthy to take one attribute and concentrate on it while ignoring the rest.

God's love is not a one-way street; it calls for accountability, and that is where God's holiness comes in. God's holiness is non-negotiable; it exists whether we want it to or not. Sinners like us can't stand in God's presence except through the person and work of Jesus Christ. The moment of decision only exists for those who are alive; after death comes judgment. We must not buy into a simplistic message that tells us what we want to hear. Such messages promise churchgoers health and wealth without tackling the problem of sin. At the final judgment, God will judge everyone's actions in relation to how we responded to the sacrifice of his Son.

Yes, God is love, but he is also holy, and if we chose to continue living in sin, we'll have no share in his kingdom both now and in the age to come. Wishful thinking won't make the future judgment go away; it won't make God look the other way out of love. Jesus Christ is our only hope for a verdict of "non-guilty" on that final day! The best news of all is that those of us who belong to Jesus Christ can hear and experience that verdict spoken over us right now in the present: "Therefore, since we have been justified by faith, we have peace with God through our Lord Jesus Christ" (Rom. 5:1).

Luke: The Final Judgment and Eternal Reward and Punishment

As with Matthew, Luke gives more attention to the final judgment than to the coming of the Son of Man or the future resurrection. This theme in Jesus' teaching served an ethical purpose to motivate Jesus' hearers to repent in the knowledge that they would be held accountable for their actions.

Final Judgment, Reward, and Punishment in Luke

1. "Woe to you, Chorazin! Woe to you, Bethsaida! For if the mighty works done in you had been done in Tyre and Sidon, they would have repented long ago, sitting in sackcloth and ashes. But it will be more bearable in the judgment for Tyre and Sidon than for you.

And you, Capernaum, will you be exalted to heaven? You shall be brought down to Hades." (Luke 10:13–15)

2. "The queen of the South will rise up at the judgment with the men of this generation and condemn them, for she came from the ends of the earth to hear the wisdom of Solomon, and behold, something greater than Solomon is here. The men of Nineveh will rise up at the judgment with this generation and condemn it, for they repented at the preaching of Jonah, and behold, something greater than Jonah is here." (Luke 11:31–32)

3. "But I will warn you whom to fear: fear him who, after he has killed, has authority to cast into hell. Yes, I tell you, fear him!" (Luke 12:5)

4. "And I tell you, everyone who acknowledges me before men, the Son of Man also will acknowledge before the angels of God, but the one who denies me before men will be denied before the angels of God. And everyone who speaks a word against the Son of Man will be forgiven, but the one who blasphemes against the Holy Spirit will not be forgiven." (Luke 12:8–10)

5. "But he will say, 'I tell you, I do not know where you come from. Depart from me, all you workers of evil!' In that place there will be weeping and gnashing of teeth, when you see Abraham and Isaac and Jacob and all the prophets in the kingdom of God but you yourselves cast out. And people will come from east and west, and from north and south, and recline at table in the kingdom of God. And behold, some are last who will be first, and some are first who will be last." (Luke 13:27–30)

6. "The poor man died and was carried by the angels to Abraham's side. The rich man also died and was buried, and in Hades, being in torment, he lifted up his eyes and saw Abraham far off and Lazarus at his side. And he called out, 'Father Abraham, have mercy on me, and send Lazarus to dip the end of his finger in water and cool my tongue, for I am in anguish in this flame.' But Abraham said, 'Child, remember that you in your lifetime received your good things, and Lazarus in like manner bad things; but now he is comforted here,

and you are in anguish. And besides all this, between us and you a great chasm has been fixed, in order that those who would pass from here to you may not be able, and none may cross from there to us.'" (Luke 16:22–26)

7. "And he said to them, 'Truly, I say to you, there is no one who has left house or wife or brothers or parents or children, for the sake of the kingdom of God, who will not receive many times more in this time, and in the age to come eternal life.'" (Luke 18:29–30)

8. "You are those who have stayed with me in my trials, and I assign to you, as my Father assigned to me, a kingdom, that you may eat and drink at my table in my kingdom and sit on thrones judging the twelve tribes of Israel." (Luke 22:28–30)

After our discussion on Matthew and Mark, most of these references are self-explanatory. The parable of the rich man and Lazarus indicates that Jesus could assume his hearers would agree with the reality of future judgment and punishment (16:19–31). The parable isn't told to teach his hearers about these things but to use what they already knew to be true— future judgment and punishment—to urge them to action in the present.

Truth Touches Life: A Call to Patient Waiting

How much longer must we wait for Jesus' return? Because of the prophetic urgency expressed throughout the Bible, every generation must remain alert and expectant. From the moment we enter into a personal relationship with our Lord and Savior, we have only a number of years to wait until Jesus will either return or we'll be called home. We can only wait for the Lord's return if we're still alive in this world. Our faith was handed down to us through the ages by believers who faithfully waited for the promise of the Lord's return until he called them home. These believers should be our examples, people to whom we look as a cloud of witnesses (Hebrews 11–12).

Let us therefore move forward in faith, keeping the faith and trusting in our Lord's promise to return for us. Peter elaborates on the Lord's promise: "The Lord is not slow about his promise, as some count slowness, but is patient toward you, not wishing for any to perish but for all to come to repentance" (2 Peter 3:9). Every individual Christian has a responsibility to trust and to wait for the fulfillment of our Lord's promise while he or she lives. If the Lord should return while we're still here, praise be to his name; but if we must wait and die without the fulfillment of the promise, then so be it, and we can only hope that even with our last breath we'll still be trusting his promise to return. This is what Paul joyfully described: "to live is Christ and to die is gain" (Phil. 1:21). For while we're still alive, we're alive for and in him, and when we die, we sleep with his name on our lips!

Conclusion: Resurrection and the Final Judgment

This chapter has surveyed Jesus' teaching about the resurrection and final judgment in the Synoptic Gospels. Jesus is quite traditional and endorses a widespread understanding in Judaism at that time in which there would be a resurrection followed by a final judgment. His most novel contribution in this regard is the apparently audacious claim that he himself was the Son of Man whose future coming would jumpstart these final events and he, along with God the Father, would preside over the final judgment. These were startling claims indeed and certainly part of the reason for opposition and his rejection by the Jewish religious leaders.

We'll now turn our attention to John's Gospel. John tells the same basic story about Jesus but includes quite a bit more teaching. He doesn't include the Olivet Discourse, but this doesn't mean he has nothing to say about the future.

Chapter 9

Jesus and the Future in John's Gospel

In the previous chapters, we've seen that Matthew, Mark, and Luke reveal that, regarding the near future, Jesus prophesied that there would be (1) persecution of his followers and (2) a judgment of "this generation" with special attention on the Jewish religious leadership for their rejection of him. Regarding the more distant future, we've seen that Jesus taught that (3) the Son of Man will come with power; (4) and there will be a future resurrection and final judgment followed by eternal reward and punishment.

What does John's Gospel add to our understanding of Jesus' teaching about the future? As we'll see, John does feature these teachings of Jesus as well, except that he does not use "this generation" language. In addition, he stresses the "already" dimension of Jesus' coming—the extent to which believers can experience the benefits of salvation already in the here and now—without, however, denying the future dimension that awaits the second coming and the final consummation.[1]

What's more, John virtually omits reference to God's kingdom (except for John 3:3, 5) and instead features numerous references to eternal life. In this way, he focuses on the universal scope of Jesus' coming beyond his mission to ethnic Jews (as a reference to the Davidic kingdom may be taken to imply). Therefore, we'll see that John's account of Jesus' teaching about the future is both congruent with that contained in the other Gospels and yet significantly deepens it by broadening its scope and probing its deeper theological significance.

---

1. Scholars call this John's "realized eschatology."

Future Persecution

Jesus' teaching about the imminent future in John's Gospel contains an extended portion on the persecutions his followers would face following his crucifixion, resurrection, and ascension:

> [18] "If the world hates you, know that it has hated me before it hated you. [19] If you were of the world, the world would love you as its own; but because you are not of the world, but I chose you out of the world, therefore the world hates you. [20] Remember the word that I said to you: 'A servant is not greater than his master.' If they persecuted me, they will also persecute you. If they kept my word, they will also keep yours. [21] But all these things they will do to you on account of my name, because they do not know him who sent me. [22] If I had not come and spoken to them, they would not have been guilty of sin, but now they have no excuse for their sin. [23] Whoever hates me hates my Father also. [24] If I had not done among them the works that no one else did, they would not be guilty of sin, but now they have seen and hated both me and my Father. [25] But the word that is written in their Law must be fulfilled: 'They hated me without a cause.'
>
> [26] "But when the Helper comes, whom I will send to you from the Father, the Spirit of truth, who proceeds from the Father, he will bear witness about me. [27] And you also will bear witness, because you have been with me from the beginning.
>
> [1] "I have said all these things to you to keep you from falling away. [2] They will put you out of the synagogues. Indeed, the hour is coming when whoever kills you will think he is offering service to God. [3] And they will do these things because they have not known the Father, nor me. [4] But I have said these things to you, that when their hour comes you may remember that I told them to you." (John 15:18–16:4)

John alone among the Gospels features the "Farewell" or "Upper Room Discourse," an extended section spanning as many as five chapters in the second major half of the Gospel that contains Jesus' instructions given to his followers on the evening prior to the crucifixion. This is priceless material, especially considering that it was preserved by the one who was closest to Jesus during his earthly ministry, namely, John the apostle.[2]

Jesus' concern at this juncture was to prepare his followers for his imminent cross-death and resurrection as well as for the time after his departure to the Father, that is, his ascension and exaltation with God. Jesus tells his disciples that after his departure, the world's persecution would be transferred from him to them: "If they persecuted me, they will also persecute you" (15:20). This, in turn, can be traced back to the world's rejection of God the Father who sent Jesus: "Whoever hates me hates my Father also" (15:23).

The world's persecution of Jesus' followers, in turn, is shown to be grounded in their *election*: "If you were of the world, the world would love you as its own; but *because you are not of the world, but I chose you out of the world*, therefore the world hates you" (15:19). What's more, believers' election is followed by their *sanctification*—setting apart for God's service—and commissioning to *service* and *mission*: "*Sanctify* them in the truth; your word is truth. As you *sent* me into the world, so I have *sent* them into the world" (17:17–18; cf. 20:21–22).[3]

That said, believers will not merely be sanctified by God's Word and sent into the world, Jesus and the Father will send the Holy Spirit to undergird the disciples' witness: "But when the Helper comes, whom I will send to you from the Father, the Spirit of truth, who proceeds from the Father, he will bear witness about me. And you also will bear witness, because you have been with me from the beginning" (15:26–27). In this way, all three persons of the Godhead will empower the believing community's mission, bound together in love and unity (17:20–26).[4]

As in the other Gospels, Jesus is shown in John's Gospel to strike a realistic note: "I have said all these things to you to keep you from falling away. They will put you out of the synagogues. Indeed, the hour is coming when whoever kills you will think he is offering service to God" (16:1–2).

---

2. For a discussion of the authorship of John's Gospel, see Andreas J. Köstenberger, L. Scott Kellum, and Charles L. Quarles, *The Cradle, the Cross, and the Crown: An Introduction to the New Testament*, 2nd ed. (Nashville: B & H Academic, 2016), chap. 7.

3. On the Johannine mission theme, see Andreas J. Köstenberger, *The Missions of Jesus and the Disciples according to the Fourth Gospel* (Grand Rapids: Eerdmans, 1998).

4. See Andreas J. Köstenberger and Scott R. Swain, *Father, Son and Spirit: The Trinity and John's Gospel*, NSBT 24 (Downers Grove, IL: InterVarsity Press, 2008), esp. chap. 7.

John's Gospel includes an anticipatory glimpse of such ostracism in the case of the man born blind who progressed from physical blindness all the way to disciple and worshiper of Jesus; in the same way, his followers will be cast out of the synagogue.[5]

Escalating Conflict

While John does not feature references to "this generation" as the other biblical Gospels do, the above-cited references to the imminent persecution of his followers follow on the heels of a pattern of escalating conflict, which pervades especially chapters 5–10 of John's Gospel (the so-called Festival Cycle). Following the healing of the lame man in chapter 5, as it turned out on a Sabbath, Jesus' opponents are shown to take exception to his claim, "My Father is working until now, and I am working" (5:17). As the evangelist makes explicit, "This was why the Jews were seeking all the more to kill him, because not only was he breaking the Sabbath, but he was even calling God his own Father, making himself equal with God" (5:18).

After yet another Johannine sign, the feeding of the multitude, in chapter 6, the end of the chapter finds many of his disciples deserting him (6:60–71). Even his own brothers are shown to fail to understand the true nature of Jesus' mission at this juncture (7:1–9), though they later came to believe. The rest of chapter 7 features various messianic expectations and misconceptions held by Jesus' contemporaries. Chapters 8 and 9, too, are replete with Jesus' conflict with the Jewish authorities. Chapter 10, finally, closes the way the Festival Cycle began in chapter 5: an unequivocal identification of Jesus with God the Father—"I and the Father are one" (10:30)—promptly eliciting attempts to stone Jesus because of blasphemy (10:31).

---

5. See John 9. See the commentary on this passage in Andreas J. Köstenberger, *John*, BECNT (Grand Rapids: Baker, 2004), 276–96. Some have said the reference to synagogue expulsion in John 9 is anachronistic and relates to John's day rather than Jesus' day (e.g., the AD 90s rather than AD 30s) but there is no reason to jump to this conclusion. For a critique of the "Johannine community hypothesis," see Edward W. Kink, *The Sheep of the Fold: The Audience and Origin of the Gospel of John*, SNTSMS 141 (Cambridge: Cambridge University Press, 2007); more broadly, see Richard Bauckham, ed., *The Gospels for All Christians: Rethinking the Gospels Audiences* (Grand Rapids: Eerdmans, 1998). Note that John 16:1–2 is couched as a future prediction rather than present reality from the vantage point of the historical Jesus.

Later, when the Jewish authorities bring charges against Jesus before Pilate, the Roman governor, they reiterate, "We have a law, and according to that law he ought to die because he has made himself the Son of God" (19:7). John, more than the other Gospels, therefore makes Jesus' claim to deity and unity with God the centerpiece of his presentation of Jesus and shows that at the heart of Jewish opposition to him was the perceived offense of blasphemy. From the very outset of John's Gospel (1:1, 18) to its conclusion (20:28), Jesus is presented not merely as a good, moral teacher, or even as a divine prophet or human messianic figure, but as God incarnate who left his preexistent glory in heaven to embark on his redemptive mission and returned to the same glory once his mission was accomplished (13:1–3; 17:24; cf. 17:4; 19:30).[6]

Like the Synoptic Gospels, John focuses quite a bit on the growing conflict between Jesus and the Jewish religious leaders, but unlike the Synoptic Gospels he doesn't focus explicitly on the destruction of Jerusalem as God's judgment for rejection of the Messiah (though see the subtle references in 2:19; 4:20–21; and 11:48). This could be because John wrote a decade to two after the destruction of the temple and was more concerned to present Jesus as the replacement for the temple. His implicit argument is that Jews who formally approached and worshiped God through the temple should now approach and worship God in and through Jesus.[7]

The Son of Man

One of the most consistent elements uniting all four Gospels is Jesus referring to himself as the Son of Man. Taking its point of departure, as mentioned, from Daniel's mysterious reference to the transcendent figure of one "like a son of man" (Dan 7:13), all the Gospels show that Son of Man was Jesus' favorite self-designation, and John is certainly no exception.

Jesus' references to himself as Son of Man pervade the first half of John's Gospel, spanning from 1:51 to 13:31.[8] Remarkably, they're otherwise absent

---

6. At the heart of John's "sending Christology" is the depiction of the mission of God's Word in Isaiah, especially 55:11–12. E.g., Köstenberger, *John*, 27.

7. See especially Andreas J. Köstenberger, "The Destruction of the Second Temple and the Composition of the Fourth Gospel," in *Challenging Perspectives on the Gospel of John*, WUNT 2/219, ed. John Lierman (Tübingen: Mohr Siebeck, 2006), 69–108, and the literature cited there.

8. See chart below. Interestingly, there are no references to Jesus as the "Son of Man" in John's Letters.

from the Farewell Discourse (13:31–16:33) and the Passion Narrative (chaps. 18–20). Almost half of the Johannine instances of Son of Man form part of a cluster of references commonly called "the lifted-up sayings," involving the term *hypsoō* ("to be lifted up"), a euphemism for Jesus' cruci-fixion and subsequent resurrection (see 3:13–14; 8:28; 12:34). Otherwise, the references to Jesus as the "Son of Man" in John's Gospel bear a close resemblance to those in the Synoptics.[9]

References to the Son of Man in John's Gospel	
Reference	*Content*
1:51	The Son of Man as the locus of new divine revelation
3:13–14	First "lifted-up saying"
5:27	The Son of Man's authority to judge
6:27, 53, 62	The Son of Man's descent as the "bread of life"
8:28	Second "lifted-up saying"
9:35	Jesus' self-reference to the formerly blind man
12:23	Now is the Son of Man glorified
12:34	Third "lifted-up saying" (cf. 12:32)
13:31	Now is the Son of Man glorified

Interestingly, while the origins of Son of Man terminology are found in the apocalyptic passage of Daniel 7:13, the clear majority of these passages in John's Gospel pertains to Jesus' first coming and his redemptive mis-sion at the cross. This death at the cross, according to John, is repeatedly signaled by "lifted-up sayings" during Jesus' earthly ministry (3:14; 8:28; 12:32) and constitutes the glorification of the Son of Man (12:23). For our present purposes, the most significant Johannine references to the Son of Man are those found in 1:51 and 5:27.

In the former passage, Jesus claims to be the supreme place of divine revelation for his followers, not only at his second coming, but also during the progressive revelation of the Father that Jesus provided during his earthly ministry at his first coming. This has very important implications

---

9. The following discussion of the Johannine treatment of the "Son of Man" is adapted from Andreas J. Köstenberger, *A Theology of John's Gospel and Letters: The Word, the Christ, the Son of God*, BTNT (Grand Rapids: Zondervan, 2009), §20.4.

for believers today, as it directs them to consider the many ways in which Jesus revealed God the Father already during the time he spent on earth.

A sampling of relevant passages from John's Gospel bears this out:

- John 1:18: "No one has ever seen God; the only God, who is at the Father's side, he has made him known."
- John 5:19: "Whatever the Father does, that the Son does likewise."
- John 14:9: "Whoever has seen me has seen the Father."

Rather than being unduly preoccupied with the circumstances surrounding Jesus' future second coming, believers should therefore make every effort to grow in their personal knowledge and relationship with Jesus by following his teaching and obeying his directions (8:31; 15:14).

Equally if not even more important for our present purposes is the reference to Jesus as the Son of Man at 5:27. We've already taken a brief look at this passage in the survey of Johannine references to the Son of Man above. Because the passage relates directly to the fourth topic pertaining to Jesus' teaching and role in the more distant future, we'll further discuss this reference under the next two headings.

Future Resurrection and Final Judgment

Because of John's focus on the present implications of Jesus' first coming for believers, it's sometimes alleged that John had little to no regard for the future dimension of Jesus' teaching. However, this is demonstrably false. We've already mentioned the lame man's healing and Jesus' subsequent claim of equality with God in the discussion of Jesus as the Son of Man above. It's now time to look at this passage in a bit more detail to see what it contributes to our understanding of Jesus' role in the future resurrection and the final judgment.

> [19] So Jesus said to them, "Truly, truly, I say to you, the Son can do nothing of his own accord, but only what he sees the Father doing. For whatever the Father does, that the Son does likewise. [20] For the Father loves the Son and shows him all that he himself is doing. And greater works than these will he show him, so that you may marvel. [21] *For as the Father raises the dead and gives them life, so also the Son gives life to whom he will.* [22] *For the Father*

judges no one, but has given all judgment to the Son, [23] that all may
honor the Son, just as they honor the Father. Whoever does not
honor the Son does not honor the Father who sent him. [24] Truly,
truly, I say to you, whoever hears my word and believes him who
sent me has eternal life. He does not come into judgment, but has
passed from death to life.

[25] "Truly, truly, I say to you, an hour is coming, and is now
here, when the dead will hear the voice of the Son of God, and
those who hear will live. [26] For as the Father has life in himself, so
he has granted the Son also to have life in himself. [27] *And he has
given him authority to execute judgment, because he is the Son of
Man.* [28] *Do not marvel at this, for an hour is coming when all who
are in the tombs will hear his voice* [29] *and come out, those who have
done good to the resurrection of life, and those who have done evil to
the resurrection of judgment."* (John 5:19–29)

While a distinction is clearly maintained between Father and Son—
they are distinct persons—it is also clear that at the same time Jesus asserts
parity with God by claiming to have life in himself, being able to raise the
dead, and serving as the agent of resurrection and final judgment following his second coming. The assertions in the above-cited passage are largely
self-explanatory; nevertheless, they're truly remarkable in that they affirm
that Jesus has a unique role, not only at his first coming but at his second
coming as well.

It is here, then, that John's emphasis on the present reality of events
typically consigned to the future (his "realized eschatology") comes to the
fore. Both Jesus' activity of raising the dead and his role as the end-time
judge are shown to be on display already during the time of his earthly
ministry. The raising of Lazarus, the seventh and climactic sign in John's
Gospel, found only in this Gospel (11:1–44), may serve as an example.[10]
In the narrative scheme of the Gospel, it anticipates and paves the way for
Jesus' own resurrection later in the Gospel.

In addition, the account serves as an acted-out demonstration of two
views of eschatology: the conventional Jewish schema of the two ages—the

---

10. On the Johannine signs, see Andreas J. Köstenberger, "The Seventh Johannine
Sign: A Study in John's Christology," *BBR* 5 (1995): 87–103.

present age and the age to come—which also predominates the Synoptic Gospels and the Johannine schema in which these two ages are to some extent collapsed, or perhaps better, in which the age to come is shown to already have decisively invaded the present age. So when Jesus is on the way to raise Lazarus from the dead, he tells the dead man's sister, Martha, "Your brother will rise again" (11:23).

Martha replies, representative of conventional Jewish eschatology, "I know that he will rise again *in the resurrection on the last day*" (11:24; emphasis added). Then Jesus says to her, "I am the resurrection and the life. Whoever believes in me, though he die, yet shall he live, and everyone who lives and believes in me shall never die. Do you believe this?" (11:25–26). At this, Martha retorts, "Yes, Lord, I believe that you are the Christ, the Son of God, who is coming into the world" (11:27), remarkably uttering a confession that anticipates John's later purpose statement (20:30–31).

Martha is telling Jesus that Lazarus will rise in the age to come, but Jesus is telling her he is going to raise Lazarus *right now*! The message is clear: There's no need for believers to think of eschatology as exclusively a matter of the future. Rather, in Jesus, the end times are already upon us! Whoever believes in him has *already* entered the age to come, although it's of course still true that only following his second coming will the presence of sin, death, and suffering be removed (Rev. 21:4).

The same is true regarding the final judgment. Rather than relegating it to the time following Jesus' second coming, John characterizes Jesus as saying, "Truly, truly, I say to you, whoever hears my word and believes him who sent me has eternal life. He does not come into judgment, but has passed from death to life" (5:24). In other words, the person who believes in Jesus as Messiah already has eternal life in the here and now. He has *already* "passed from death to life" (past tense)!

The actual time of judgment, John avers, is already in the here and now: "Whoever believes in him [Jesus] is not condemned, but whoever does not believe *is condemned already*, because he has not believed in the name of the only Son of God" (3:18). Later in John's Gospel, toward the middle, Jesus asserts, "Now is the judgment of this world; now will the ruler of this world be cast out" (12:31). Again, John stresses the present reality of God's judgment effected by Jesus' first coming, in this case the judgment of the devil ("the ruler of this world") through Jesus' death on the cross.

Preparing a Place in the Father's House

In addition, we find in John's Gospel some comforting teachings by Jesus about the future. Among these, none is better known or more significant than that found in John 14:1–3:

> [1] "Let not your hearts be troubled. Believe in God; believe also in me. [2] In my Father's house are many rooms. If it were not so, would I have told you that I go to prepare a place for you? [3] And if I go and prepare a place for you, I will come again and will take you to myself, that where I am you may be also.

This is significant information for how believers will spend their future. The passage certainly contradicts the contention that John knows little to nothing about the future dimension of eschatology. Here Jesus is telling his followers that he is about to depart to prepare a dwelling place for them in heaven and that after this he promises them to "come again" and to take them to be with him forever.

In Jesus' day, people often combined multiple dwelling units into a large, extended household. Customarily, sons added to their father's house once married. In this way, the family estate grew into a large compound, often centered in a communal courtyard. In addition, the passage may conjure up notions of luxurious Greco-Roman villas, including shady trees and flowing water.[11]

Just as Jesus' first disciples asked him where he was staying and told them to "come and see" (1:38–39), he now assures them that he won't relinquish his responsibility to provide for them. What's more, his provision of eternal dwellings for them transposes this theme onto a higher plane. Jesus here stresses that there'll be plenty of room in heaven and that "believers' future is bound up with a homecoming comparable to a son's return to his father's house."[12]

---

11. For further details and bibliographic and primary references see Köstenberger, *John*, 425–27; idem, "John," in *Zondervan Illustrated Bible Backgrounds Commentary*, vol. 2, ed. Clinton E. Arnold (Grand Rapids: Zondervan, 2001), 137–38.

12. Köstenberger, *John*, 427. Cf. the parable of the prodigal son in Luke 15:11–32. The rendering "mansions" rather than "rooms" crept into English versions through Tyndale (1526) by way of the Latin Vulgate (*mansio*), though the meaning of "mansion" has changed over time, so "rooms" is a better rendering than "mansion" in the present passage

Jesus' going to prepare a place for his followers is reminiscent of the pattern of Deuteronomy where God is shown to go ahead and prepare a place for his people in the Promised Land (see, e.g., 1:29–33).[13] Similarly, Jesus is depicted in the book of Hebrews as a "forerunner" who has finished his course and entered heaven (6:20; 12:2), and reference is made to a "heavenly country" or "city" prepared for believers (11:16).

Then, after preparing a place for believers, Jesus promises to come again, clearly a reference to the second coming (cf. John 21:22–23).[14] The terminology is reminiscent of the language used in the Song of Solomon, where the bride says she will bring her groom to her mother's house (Song 8:2). Here Jesus, the messianic bridegroom (cf. John 3:29), is said to go to prepare a place for his own in his Father's house and then to come to take them home with him.[15] This imagery beautifully anticipates the depiction of the wedding supper of the Lamb in the book of Revelation (19:6–9).

Resurrection and New Creation

John's Gospel opens with an unmistakable reference to God's original creation and the Word's participation in it (1:1–3).[16] This opening sets the framework for the remainder of the Gospel, that is, creation theology in which to place the coming of Jesus as the incarnate Word. It also shows that Jesus' coming has implications far beyond merely the Jewish people, extending to the entire cosmos (the "world"). As the so-called universal Gospel, John transcends predominantly Jewish categories such as "kingdom" and replaces these with expressions such as "life," "light," and

---

(cf. Carson, *Gospel according to John*, 489). Sorry to those who were looking forward to living in a mansion in heaven! We're sure our eternal dwellings will still surpass anything we can imagine, and more importantly, God himself will be there and we'll live in his presence forever!

13. See especially Peter W. L. Walker, *Jesus and the Holy City: New Testament Perspectives on Jerusalem* (Grand Rapids: Eerdmans, 1996), 186–90, esp. 188.

14. See the interaction with the opposing views by Schnackenburg and Keener in Köstenberger, *John*, 427, n. 30.

15. Elsewhere in John, "my Father's house" refers to the Jerusalem Temple (2:16; cf. Luke 2:49). Thus, some have alleged that John 14:2–3 likewise refers to the ancient conception of heaven as God's temple. This is possible, but not likely. Contra J. McCaffrey, *The House with Many Rooms: The Temple Theme of Jn. 14,2–3*, AnBib 114 (Rome: Pontifical Bible Institute, 1988).

16. This section adapts portions from chapter 8 in Köstenberger, *Theology of John's Gospel and Letters*.

"world." In this way, John seeks to demonstrate that Jesus' coming encompasses all of human history, both temporally and spatially.

What's more, the initial creation setting in John's Gospel is carried forward by the presentation of the first week of Jesus' ministry in possible analogy to the first week of creation and the discussion of the new birth in Jesus' conversation with Nicodemus (in further development of 1:12–13). While the initial references to creation in the introduction pertain primarily to God's original creation in and through Jesus "the Word," the Passion Narrative toward the end of the Gospel builds on these references and sets Jesus' crucifixion and resurrection within the context of a new creation.

There are several possible indications for the presence of such "new creation theology" in the Passion Narrative, including the following:

- Its setting in a garden (18:1, 26; 19:41; this is a unique to John)
- Pilate's identification of Jesus as "the Man" (19:5), which may identify Jesus as the "new Adam," a possible instance of word play and Johannine irony
- The casting of Jesus' resurrection as the beginning of a new creation (20:1; cf. 1:3)[17]
- The identification of Jesus as "the gardener" by Mary (20:15), reflecting misunderstanding and possibly irony as well
- Jesus' bodily resurrection and appearances to his followers in keeping with repeated predictions earlier in the Johannine narrative (chap. 20; cf. 2:20–21; 10:17–19)
- Jesus' breathing on his disciples and giving of the Spirit in the final commissioning scene (20:22), invoking the creation of Adam in Gen 2:7 (cf. Ezek. 37:9)[18]

From the first verse (18:1) to the final chapter, therefore, the Johannine Passion Narrative reverberates with new creation theology, harking back

---

17. See Derek Tidball, "Completing the Circle: The Resurrection according to John," *Evangelical Review of Theology* 30 (2006): 169–83.

18. See Jan A. DuRand, "The Creation Motif in the Fourth Gospel: Perspectives on Its Narratological Function within a Judaistic Background," in *Theology and Christology in the Fourth Gospel: Essays by the Members of the SNTS Johannine Writings Seminar*, ed. G. Van Belle, J. G. Van der Watt, and P. Maritz (Leuven: Leuven University Press, 2005), 21–46, esp. 43–46.

to the opening references to the original creation in the introduction to the Gospel. By this John seeks to imply that salvation through faith in Jesus as Messiah anticipates the consummation of human history in the new creation. It further means that John's Gospel is the Gospel equivalent to the Johannine Apocalypse, which likewise ends with the end-time consummation of what began in the Garden of Eden in the New Jerusalem.

In this regard, it's also significant that the entire Gospel is pervaded by references to life—"eternal life," which those who believe in Jesus receive, as well as "light" and "darkness" symbolism. Also, the anticipation of the giving of the Spirit finds expression several times in the Gospel, from sporadic initial references (3:34; 7:39) to the mounting promise of the Spirit's coming following Jesus' exaltation in chapters 14–16 and the Spirit's symbolic impartation in 20:22. In this way, John makes clear throughout his narrative that life in the Spirit will characterize the experience of believers in Jesus once he has been exalted to the Father.

Another possible instance of new creation theology in John's Gospel is the reference to "the first day of the week" in 20:1 and 19 and to the phrase "after eight days" in 20:26 in conjunction with references to Jesus "completing his work" in 19:28, 30.[19] It's clear from John's Gospel that Jesus came to complete his Father's work (see esp. 5:17). In fact, as noted, Jesus performed several of his "signs" on the Sabbath (e.g., 5:9b, 17; 9:3–4, 14). While per Genesis 2:2, God rested from all his work on the seventh day, now Jesus, on the eighth day, resumed and completed God's work. Thus, following the cross, God's eternal Sabbath can begin (19:31; 20:1).

Perhaps most importantly, the new creation theology of John's Gospel climaxes in the resurrection of the Word-made-flesh, the lifted-up Son of Man, and the suffering Servant. As Creator and Sender, Jesus breathes life into his new messianic community and commissions his followers to proclaim the message of forgiveness and eternal life through believing in

---

19. Cf. 17:4, which forms an *inclusio* with 4:34. Cf. Jeannine K. Brown ("Creation's Renewal in the Gospel of John," *CBQ* 72 [2010]: 275–90), who also contends that the resurrection is the eighth Johannine "sign," also forming a part in John's "new creation theology." This is one of the few unpersuasive elements of Brown's article, since the resurrection doesn't seem to fit the Johannine conception of a "sign." Instead, it is the reality to which the "signs" point and cannot therefore itself be a sign as well. See Köstenberger, "Seventh Johannine Sign."

Jesus (20:22). In this way, John's narrative builds inexorably from creation to new creation, spanning the entire range from preexistent, glorious Word to the enfleshed Word's return to its preexistent glory following its death, burial, and resurrection. Thus, the Isaianic pattern of the divine Word's mission has been fulfilled in Jesus, the Messiah and Son of God (Isa. 55:11). In the logic of John's narrative, the resurrection of Jesus constitutes the central plank.[20]

New creation theology in John's Gospel, in turn, sets the universal stage for the salvation-historical drama pitting the Christ against Satan and the unbelieving world. Against a cosmic backdrop, John shows that Jesus epitomized true Israel and fulfilled the symbolism underlying the nation's religious observances. This comprises the Law—including the Sabbath—as well as the temple, and festivals such as Passover, Tabernacles, and Dedication. Jesus is the new and true Israel (the "vine," 15:1), while his "own" are the believing remnant, who place their faith in him as Messiah (13:1; cf. 1:11). Therefore, the Johannine drama of the glorified Christ plays out in cosmic proportions, while at the same time encompassing the salvation-historical dimension of the Messiah coming to Israel whose rejection of Christ opens the way for believing Gentiles to be incorporated into the new messianic community.

Conclusion

We've seen that John's account of Jesus' teaching about the future both coheres with that of the other Gospels while at the same time considerably deepening our understanding in this regard. Like the other Gospels, John affirms that Jesus spoke to his followers about coming times of persecution. While not using "this generation" language, John, too, presents these persecutions as part of a trajectory of escalating conflict between Jesus and his opponents, which would culminate in Jesus himself replacing the Jerusalem temple. John's teaching regarding Jesus as the Son of Man is likewise entirely consistent with that found in the other Gospels, including Jesus' role as the eschatological judge and as the end-time agent of the final resurrection.

---

20. For a collection of essays on various aspects of Jesus' resurrection in John's Gospel, see *The Resurrection of Jesus in the Gospel of John*, ed. Craig R. Koester and Reimund Bieringer, WUNT 222 (Tübingen: Mohr-Siebeck, 2008).

At the same time, we've seen that John, more than the other Gospels, draws out the eschatological implications of Jesus' first coming more fully, showing that we needn't simply wait for the second coming to experience the end-time benefits of Jesus' coming. In this vein, John asserts that believers in Jesus have eternal life already in the here and now, in keeping with Jesus' purpose: "I came that they may have life and have it abundantly" (John 10:10). Also, the time to escape God's wrath at the final judgment is in this present life. Those who have believed in Jesus will not come into judgment on the final day, while those who reject Jesus are condemned already. The final judgment will simply pronounce the final verdict.

What's more, essentially God's judgment on people is self-inflicted in that people bring it upon themselves by rejecting Jesus' sacrifice on their behalf at the cross. John makes an important clarification in 3:36: "Whoever believes in the Son has eternal life; whoever does not obey the Son shall not see life, but the wrath of God remains on him." It's therefore not true that unbelievers are in a neutral position regarding God; rather, unless they place their faith in Jesus, God's wrath already rests on them. While this may not seem fair to modern sensibilities, it's a consequence of all of humanity sharing in the sin of Adam, the first human being (Rom. 5:12; cf. Rom. 3:23).

Finally, we've seen how John presents Jesus' coming in terms of his inauguration of the new creation. In the beginning was the Word, and nothing was made without the Word (1:1–3). Jesus' first week of ministry is cast as equivalent to the seven days of creation. Jesus' resurrection—in a garden, no less—is followed by his commissioning of the new messianic community by breathing on it his Spirit (20:22), anticipating the announcement at the end of the book of Revelation, "Behold, I am making all things new" (Rev. 21:5). Amazingly, in Jesus, this new creation has already begun. It has already been inaugurated at his first coming and is moving inexorably toward its consummation at his second coming. In the interim, he calls us to follow him until he comes (John 21:19, 22–23).

The bottom line, then, is this: We must trust in Jesus in the here and now so that we will receive eternal life and escape eternal judgment. This is the message of John's Gospel from the beginning purpose statement (1:12) to the closing purpose statement (20:30–31) and everywhere in between (esp. 3:16). If you're reading these words and you're a believer, you can walk with Jesus closely as a branch is integrally related to and nurtured by the vine (John 15:1–11) and live by his teachings, which is the mark of a true disciple of Jesus (8:31). If you haven't yet believed, please consider the claims of Jesus and the promise for believing in God's Son, forgiveness of sins and eternal life—an eternity spent in the presence of our good and loving Creator and Savior of our souls! How could anyone turn down such an irresistible offer?

Conclusion of Part 2

Part 2 surveyed Jesus' teaching about the future outside of the Olivet Discourse in the Gospels. We noted that Jesus discusses two main topics regarding the *immediate* future: (1) his followers will be persecuted and (2) the current generation will be judged by the destruction of Jerusalem and the temple. The first of these began rather quickly and has applied to Jesus' followers throughout history. The second of these was fulfilled in the year 70.

In addition to the near future, Jesus also prophesied and taught about the *distant* future: (3) after a long unspecific period of time, Jesus will visibly and physically come again in glory with the angels; (4) the resurrection and final judgment will lead to eternal salvation in God's kingdom for God's people and punishment for unbelievers. These four broad topics summarize Jesus' teaching about the future in our four canonical Gospels. They also cohere with his teaching on the future in the Olivet Discourse (Part 1).

Depending on your expectations, Jesus' teaching may have produced a few surprises. First, Jesus spends far more time and energy on the *near* future events of the year 70 than is commonly recognized. Since these events are in the past from our perspective, they may not seem important but they were certainly important from the perspective of Jesus and his first followers. One problem is that people often try to find clues about the distant future from the things Jesus said concerning the near-future events of the year 70. To be sure, there's a typological connection in which the judgment and destruction of Jerusalem in the year 70 point forward to and foreshadow the future judgment, but the two events are distinct.

Second, Jesus is quite sparse in his description of *distant* future events (though he does include two telling similes in Luke 17:26–30). He endorses the common understanding in Judaism as we assume it to be at the time in which there would be a resurrection followed by a final judgment. His most novel contribution in this regard is the audacious claim that he himself was the Son of Man whose future coming would trigger these final events and he, along with God the Father, would preside over the final judgment. These were startling claims indeed and part of the reason for opposition and his rejection by the Jewish religious leaders.

Depending on your expectations, several elements are conspicuously absent from Jesus' teaching about the future. He doesn't teach about the rebuilding of the temple following the destruction of the year 70. From Jesus' perspective, the destruction of the temple would be final; the earliest Christians recognized this and relatively quickly made the shift to speaking about God's people as the temple for the indwelling Holy Spirit.[21] Jesus doesn't explicitly teach about a personal anti-Christ, a rapture, a seven-year period of tribulation, a millennium, or the restoration of the Jewish nation after the events of the year 70. Interpreters may point to hints of these things but they are nowhere explicit.[22] We aren't claiming that these ideas are absent from the entire Bible but that one will not find explicit references to them in Jesus' teaching. Jesus gave a sign and timeframe for the destruction of Jerusalem but regarding his future coming stressed an unspecified period of time between his departure and eventual return and the unexpected nature of the coming. The period of waiting would be so long that many would be lulled to sleep, a complacent contentment with the status quo, and lack of desire for Jesus' return. The unexpected nature of the timing of the coming forms the basis for Jesus' repeated warnings for his followers to remain constantly alert, vigilant, and active in the work of the kingdom.

From Jesus' perspective, the events of the end times were rather straightforward: After a lengthy period (the length of which was unknowable), he would return visibly and physically in glory with his angels to inaugurate the future resurrection and participate with the Father in the final judgment that would lead to final salvation in God's kingdom for his people and punishment for all others. This scenario is consistent in all four Gospels, even though, of course, we also noted some distinctive emphases in each Gospel.

---

21. 1 Corinthians 3:16–17; 6:19; 2 Corinthians 6:16; Ephesians 2:21–22; 1 Timothy 3:15; Hebrews 3:6.

22. Matthew 19:28 and Luke 22:28–30 are sometimes cited in support of some of these items, but see the discussion of these passages in chapter 8.

Epilogue

If you've carefully worked through the discussion in the earlier chapters, you know what Jesus taught about the future, both the immediate and the more distant future. What Jesus said matters because he's our authority in all matters of faith and practice. That's why we believe that for anyone who wants to know what the Bible says about the future, looking at Jesus is a great place to start. In fact, it's the proper place to start, if not the only proper one. Therefore, we looked first and foremost at the major body of teaching Jesus provided on the end times—the Olivet Discourse—in all three Gospels in which it is found as well as at other teachings of Jesus in these Gospels, plus in the Gospel of John on the same subject.

We've tried to leave no stone unturned to identify Jesus' essential teachings on the future both in terms of specific passages and in terms of major thematic strands common to the Gospels. We believe that our study can serve as an important corrective to much popular thinking and writing on the subject that focuses primarily on the distant future. As we've seen, Jesus in fact spent a significant amount of time talking about the more *immediate* future, urging believers to persevere under persecution, calling them to remain alert and vigilant as the culture around them will gradually deteriorate, and affirming that believers can enjoy eternal and abundant life *now* and pass from judgment into life *now* rather than having to wait for an unspecified time until his return. All of this is exceedingly helpful as it shows us how to live in the present *in view of the future*, cognizant of the fact that in many ways the future has invaded the present and, in the Holy Spirit, is already here.

And yet, as any biblically aware person knows, the Bible and the New Testament contain more than the four Gospels. Regarding the Old Testament, we've shown that Jesus picked up many elements and applied them to himself and the future, such as Daniel's figure of the Son of Man. In addition, the Old Testament contains other teachings on the future that we couldn't cover adequately (or at all) in the present volume.

The New Testament, likewise, continues past the Gospels. There are Paul's letters, thirteen in all, several of them containing vital teachings on the end times, such as Romans 9–11 on the future of ethnic Israel or 1 Thessalonians 4:13–17 on the so-called rapture. We did touch on the latter passage briefly as it contains multiple echoes of Jesus' Olivet Discourse, though space didn't permit (and our focus precluded) dealing with the former passage and other relevant Pauline passages, including his teaching on the resurrection and the nature of the resurrection body in 1 Corinthians 15. Then there are the so-called General Epistles that contain additional teaching on the end times, such as 2 Peter 3 warning against taking a supposed delay in the Lord's return as evidence that the teaching regarding his return is a mere myth.

Finally, there is the quintessential book about the end times, the Apocalypse, or book of Revelation. This is the final bookend of the entire Bible, showing the conclusion of history parallel to the beginning of history at creation (the book of Genesis). The book contains four visions the apostle John was given by God while in exile on the island of Patmos. Again, if our goal had been to canvass all the scriptural teaching on the end times, the book of Revelation would have needed to be given extensive treatment. That said, there are already several excellent commentaries on this important book of Scripture.[1]

Hermeneutically speaking, it's important to note that a study of Jesus' teaching is only a partial exploration of the subject. At the same time, we should point out that Jesus is at the heart of human history, and his teaching on this as on any subject should provide the point of departure for any Bible-believing Christian. Therefore, we humbly present our findings regarding Jesus' teachings on the future so you can move on to study this subject in the remainder of the New Testament using other Bible study tools. Not that everyone agrees on the subject; far from it. In fact, even the authors of this volume don't agree on everything pertaining to the subject of eschatology. That said, we decided to meet on the common ground of Scripture and to use the most proven methods of biblical interpretation of

---

1. See the bibliography at the end of chapter 20 in Andreas J. Köstenberger, L. Scott Kellum, and Charles L. Quarles, *The Cradle, the Cross, and the Crown: An Introduction to the New Testament*, 2nd ed. (Nashville: B & H Academic, 2016); and see the entire chapter for a thorough discussion of introductory matters to the book.

which we are aware to discern inductively, as much as humanly possible, what these teachings are.[2] In addition, we accessed other people's learned commentaries where appropriate to learn from the diligent study of others.

We realize that we're not answering every question you may have regarding the future. There are limits to what we can know based on what Jesus (and the other biblical writers, under divine inspiration) have chosen to reveal. But while God chose not to answer all our questions on this or other subjects in Scripture, he has given us all we need to know to live a godly life in the here and now.[3] We know that we must *trust in Jesus*. He is the way, the truth, and the life. He gave his life as a ransom for many when he died for us on the cross. Even when we don't know the answer, and we don't know what the future holds, we can trust him. He will never leave us. He will never let us down. And he will always love us.

We also know that we must be both *faithful* and *vigilant*. Whether Jesus should return before or after the Great Tribulation, we must be ready whenever he appears to take us with him. This is the lesson Jesus sought to impart when telling the parable of the ten virgins and other similar parables. Are you, and are we, ready for his return? If not, what must we do to get ready? We should live lives of quiet faithfulness. We should devote ourselves to our God-given calling, our work, our families, and whatever else God has called us to be and do in the few short years he has given us on this earth. If you're a believer, your eternal destiny has already been decided. But what about others?

Even though sin has distorted God's image in us, and our ancient foe, the devil, is still seeking to work us woe, God, in Christ, has launched a massive restoration project. Think of restoring Michelangelo's Sistine Chapel to bring out once again the beautiful colors—dark red, aqua blue, bright yellow—that had been buried under centuries of corrosion. What

---

2. For a recent book on this topic, see R. Alan Fuhr and Andreas J. Köstenberger, *Inductive Bible Study: Observation, Interpretation, and Application through the Lenses of History, Literature, and Theology* (Nashville: B & H Academic, 2016); see also Andreas J. Köstenberger and Richard D. Patterson, *Invitation to Biblical Interpretation* (Grand Rapids: Kregel, 2011).

3. See especially 2 Peter 1:3–11, which states that God has given us everything we need to live a godly live through our relationship with Jesus Christ. For an exposition of this passage and a discussion of the pursuit of Christian virtues, see Andreas J. Köstenberger, *Excellence: The Character of God and the Pursuit of Scholarly Virtue* (Wheaton, IL: Crossway, 2011).

God is in the process of accomplishing in Christ in those who have placed their trust in him makes restoring the Sistine Chapel pale by comparison. We're called to reflect God's glory—his beauty, his wisdom, his goodness, his love—in the lives we live and in the relationships we nurture and pursue. Like a beautiful stained-glass window, we're called to refract the rays of the sun—or, in our case, the Son. Both by whetting the appetite of unbelievers and making the gospel attractive, and by giving a reasoned defense of the hope within us, we're called to advance God's kingdom on earth and to contribute to his greater glory. This is our mandate from him as we eagerly and expectantly wait for his return.

Cosmic Upheaval in the Old Testament

In chapter 3, we briefly discussed the Old Testament background to Jesus' language of cosmic upheaval and noted that this language was generally used to poetically describe the destruction of a major city as an earthshaking catastrophe. The language of cosmic upheaval (earthquakes, storms, darkness, and fire) stresses the theophanic (God-revealing) nature of the event: God is actively present and involved in bringing the judgment. The execution of the judgment, however, is generally fulfilled by the more mundane means of human armies. Some interpreters suggest that Jesus uses the language of cosmic upheaval in the Olivet Discourse in the same way as the Old Testament prophets to describe the destruction of Jerusalem in the year 70.

We argued in chapter 3 that this is not the case, but we also think that it is helpful for readers to consider the Old Testament background for themselves. Appendix 1 will discuss most of the Old Testament passages that include the language of cosmic upheaval to describe God's activity in judging nations. We don't provide the full text of the passages discussed, so it will be important to have a Bible at hand to benefit from the following discussion. Descriptions of cosmic upheaval fall within a larger category of disaster and judgment language used by the prophets in the Hebrew Scriptures.

It's not immediately evident whether this language of cosmic upheaval is intended to be understood literally or figuratively in the New Testament documents, including the Olivet Discourse and the book of Revelation. For example, do these prophesies literally predict that the sun and moon will someday go dark and the stars will fall from the sky? To lay the foundation for a better understanding of the nature of this language in the New

Testament, this Appendix will discuss the vocabulary of disaster within the writing prophets of the Hebrew Scriptures. Even though the Hebrew writing prophets ministered over hundreds of years in various contexts, they were united in their pronouncements of divine judgment by shared motifs involving a theophany (appearance of God) generally associated with earthquakes, storms, darkness, and fire.

Before the actual texts are examined, we should comment on the relationship of theophanic disaster language in the Hebrew prophets to historic theophanies. The record of Yahweh's theophanic appearances to the Israelites in cloud and fire in the exodus (Exod. 13:21–22) and his appearance on Sinai with thunder, lightning, smoke, thick cloud, fire, and earthquake (Exod. 19:9–18; 20:18–21) made an unforgettable impression on the Hebrew people.[1] Other accounts of theophanies, both before and after Sinai, reinforce the perception of God's presence in the world to judge and save being accompanied by storms, fire, and general cosmic upheaval.[2]

Apart from the visionary callings of Isaiah and Ezekiel, the prophetic literature does not contain literal, historical theophanies. The theophanies discussed by the Hebrew prophets are either recollections of past theophanies or visions and prophecies of future theophanies when Yahweh would intervene in history to judge and save, often associated with the day of the Lord.[3] Habakkuk 3 is a clear recollection of the Sinai theophany with the prayer of Habakkuk that God would act that way again in the present (v. 2) and a resignation to wait in hope for God to thus act (vv.16–19).

---

1. Jeffrey Jay Niehaus, *God at Sinai: Covenant and Theophany in the Bible and Ancient Near East* (Grand Rapids: Zondervan, 1995), 195–200.

2. Niehaus, *God at Sinai,* discusses the accounts of theophanies in Genesis 1:2, 27–30; 2:15–17; 3:8; 15:12–18; Exodus 3:1–4:17; 13:21–22; 33:9–11; 40:34–35; Leviticus 10:2; Numbers 11:1–3; 12:5–10; 14:10–21; 16:19–32; Joshua 5:13–15; Judges 6:11–18, 19–24; 13:10–20; 1 Kings 8:6–13; 19:11–18; Isaiah 6:1–13; Ezekiel 1:1–3:15; 3:23–24; 8:2–4.

3. Niehaus (ibid., 281), divides all Old Testament theophanies not portraying actual appearances of God into three categories: "evocative recollections of the *magdalia Dei* of the Exodus and wilderness wanderings; imaginative portrayals of God's Sinai-like coming (to save the suppliant, or to judge Israel and the nations); and eschatological portrayals of God's return to judge the nations and save his people." Most of the texts studied below will fall into the second category of imaginative portrayals of God's appearance in judgment while a few of the texts may be genuinely eschatological.

Much of the language of disaster in the prophetic literature pictures God at work in the world, bringing justice in judgment on sin, idolatry, rebellion, and wickedness. Theophanic language (earthquakes, storms, darkness, and fire) is used since God is personally at work in the judgment. While this awareness is crucial, it does not by itself answer the question as to whether the theophanic vocabulary of disaster in the prophets is literal or figurative. We cannot assume that all such language is automatically figurative because Yahweh literally appeared and acted in such a way in the past during the exodus and at Sinai. When God visits his creation, such cosmic upheaval should be literally expected!

Isaiah 5:8–30

A series of six woe oracles fill this section and give the reasons for God's anger against Israel.[4] Because they have rejected his law and despised his word, Yahweh's anger was kindled against them (vv. 24–25a). He struck them, the mountains quaked, and their corpses filled the streets. This description is followed by a description of Yahweh whistling for a foreign army (v. 26). The army comes and is swift and powerful (vv. 26–30). When the army comes, one looking at the land sees darkness and distress and the light is darkened by clouds (v. 30). The theophanic elements of the outpouring of God's anger in this section (earthquake, darkness, loss of light, clouds) are figurative and are fulfilled by the description of the invading army. A physical, historical army fulfills the theophanic imagery.

Isaiah 9:19

Through the wrath of Yahweh, the land will be burned and the people will be fuel for the fire. The fulfillment of this theophanic fire scorching the land is further described as the brothers Manasseh, Ephraim, and Judah killing and feeding on each other (9:19–21 [9:18–20]). The pouring out of God's theophanic fire is figurative and historically fulfilled by the Syro-Ephraimite war (735–732 BC).

---

4. Brevard S. Childs, *Isaiah*, OTL (Louisville: Westminster John Knox Press, 2001), 46, argues it is directed against Judah and Jerusalem. For the focused nature of this Appendix it does not particularly matter. See John D. W. Watts, *Isaiah 1–33*, WBC 24 (Waco, TX: Word, 1985), 60 for arguments in favor of Israel.

Isaiah 10:16–17

Yahweh himself will kindle a burning (v. 16), will become a fire, and will burn and devour Assyria (v. 17). The description of theophanic fire imagery against Assyria is paralleled by the description of wasting disease in the ranks of his soldiers (v. 16). Watts notes, "The announcement uses Yahweh's full title, as it was used in Holy War of old. As in the old Holy War themes, the application of power is indirect. A wasting disease appropriately attacks the result of rich living in Assyrian subjects."[5] The theophanic fire is figurative and likely was fulfilled when God sent a physical wasting disease.

Isaiah 13:9–22

Isaiah decrees the coming of the day of the Lord as judgment in anger against Babylon (v. 9). The stars of heaven and their constellations will not give light, the sun will be darkened in its coming out, and the moon will not shine its light (v. 10). The heavens will tremble and the earth will quake from its place (v. 13). Babylon will never be inhabited again (v. 20). All of this is punishment for evil (v. 11) and will be carried out by the military conquest of the Medes (v. 17). The clearly theophanic imagery of the heavens and earth shaking, and going dark is figurative and is fulfilled historically by the physical armies of the Medes in military conquest of Babylon. The multiple references to Babylon (13:1, 19; 14:4, 22), the Medes (3:17), and physical warfare (13:15–18) provide a clear historical context, so this oracle should not be interpreted as a reference to the end times.[6]

Isaiah 14:16

This verse is included simply because it uses the theophanic language of the earth shaking for the military conquests of the king of Babylon. Its figurative use in this context lends support to the idea that much of the genuine theophanic shaking language in the prophets is figuratively fulfilled by human warfare.

---

5. Watts, *Isaiah 1–33*, 150.

6. Contra Childs, *Isaiah*, 124–25. Jesus' use of the language of Isaiah 13:10 in Mark 13:24–25 and Matthew 24:19 is not in the form of the fulfillment of eschatological prophecy but rather of shared vocabulary surrounding the Day of the Lord motif.

Isaiah 14:31

Like Isaiah 14:16, this verse is included because it uses the theophanic imagery of smoke coming from the north to describe a physical army coming against Philistia.[7] This is not a reference to Yahweh directly acting theophanically in judgment, but rather an example of a traditional theophanic element being used figuratively with direct physical fulfillment by human armies.

Isaiah 29:6

The interpretation of this woe oracle over Jerusalem is complicated by the ambiguity of verses 5–8. The Lord of hosts will act with thunder, earthquake, whirlwind, storm-wind, and flames of fire against either Jerusalem or the nations fighting against her. Verses 7–8 seem to indicate a grand reversal of the woe elaborated in verses 1–4 and would point to divine action against Jerusalem's foes, but the verb "punish" in verse 6 seems to be directed against Jerusalem.[8] They would be punished by these theophanic natural disasters, further described in verse 3 as a siege by foreign armies with assault towers and siege works.

Isaiah 30:27–33

This theophanic account describes God's judgment on Assyria.[9] Yahweh comes with burning anger and heavy clouds as a fire (v. 27). His breath is like a flood (v. 28), and people will hear his voice as his arm comes down with anger, flames of fire, cloudburst, rainstorm, and hail. Yahweh is depicted as fighting against Assyria with no mention of human agents, yet historically this was fulfilled by the armies of Babylon. The theophanic elements are figurative of the physical armies that devastated and destroyed Assyria.

Isaiah 34:4–17

Isaiah 34 begins with a reference to judgment against the nations but quickly focuses and remains on Edom (vv. 5–15). The hosts of heaven rot,

---

7. Smoke is used explicitly for theophanies in Isaiah 4:5 and 6:4.

8. See Watts, *Isaiah 1–33*, 378–383. Contra Childs, *Isaiah*, 217–18 and Robert B. Chisholm, *Handbook on the Prophets: Isaiah, Jeremiah, Lamentations, Ezekiel, Daniel, Minor Prophets* (Grand Rapids: Baker Academic, 2002), 74.

9. Watts, *Isaiah 1–33*, 405–406.

heaven is rolled up like a scroll, and the hosts of heaven fall (v. 4). Edom's streams are turned to pitch, her soil to sulfur, and her land to burning pitch forever (v. 9). This theophanic language of cosmic and geographic upheaval is made with no reference to human agents and has not been fulfilled literally. The streams and land of Edom have never been burning pitch and sulfur. The theophanic language of judgment, however, probably indicates the eventual destruction of Edom as a people by the Arabs.[10] If the theophanic language is interpreted figuratively, there's no need to extend the prophecy to the end times. The figurative cosmic upheaval language, the description of the streams and land turned to pitch and sulfur, and the ensuing complete abandonment (vv. 11–15) would have been fulfilled historically in military defeat and destruction as a people.

Isaiah 66:15–24

Isaiah closes with a theophanic description of judgment on all men (v. 16). Yahweh will come with fire, his chariots like the whirlwind to pour out his anger in fire (v. 15). He will execute judgment with fire and sword and many will be slain (v. 16). The fire of judgment will not be quenched in the dead bodies (v. 24). This closing theophanic account of judgment is historically undefined and not explained with historical referents. It may therefore be pointing to the end time.[11]

Jeremiah 4:3–31

Jeremiah 4 functions as a warning to the men of Judah and Jerusalem to circumcise their hearts, lest God's fury come forth like fire and burn so no one can quench it (v. 4). The Babylonian army is theophanically described as a destructive wind, and a cloud with chariots like whirlwinds (vv. 11–13). Yahweh's theophanic presence in judgment results in a reversal of creation (v. 23). The heavens had no light (v. 23), the mountains quaked, and the hills shook (v. 24). Because of all this the earth will mourn and the heavens grow dark (v. 28). There will be complete loss of inhabitants (vv. 7, 25, 29) and desolation (v. 27). The fruitful land will become a desert (v. 26). The theophanic language of judgment (earthquakes and darkened

---

10. See the helpful excursus on Edom in John D. W. Watts, *Isaiah 34–66*, WBC 25 (Waco, TX: Word, 1987), 10–11.

11. Niehaus, *God at Sinai*, 319, discusses this passage as eschatological.

sky) is figurative and is literally fulfilled by the coming Babylonian invasion.[12] This passage, more than most, describes both the invading army
(vv. 11–13) and God's judgments with theophanic vocabulary.

Jeremiah 8:16 and 10:22

The whole land shook because of the neighing of the invading horses (8:16),
and great shaking from the north will make the towns of Judah desolate.
The traditional theophanic element of "shaking" is here used figuratively
of the effects or sounds of the invading army.

Jeremiah 13:16

Jeremiah 13:16 is a warning of judgment, using theophanic imagery for
darkness. God will bring darkness, darken the hills, and turn their light
to thick darkness. The theophanic darkness is figurative of captivity (v. 17)
and exile (v. 19).

Jeremiah 15:14, 17:4, and 17:27

Yahweh's anger will kindle a fire to burn against them. Yahweh's theophanic fire of judgment is figuratively interpreted to be the enslavement of exile and captivity (15:14). Likewise, in Jeremiah 17:4 exile and captivity are
presented as the literal fulfillment of Yahweh's anger that had been kindled
and would burn forever. Jeremiah 17:27 is a warning that if people did
not honor the Sabbath, God would kindle a fire in the gates of Jerusalem
which would not be quenched and would devour the palaces of Jerusalem.
There's no mention of historical fulfillment in the immediate context, but
it is clear from elsewhere that God's threat of theophanic fire was fulfilled
with literal fire (Jer. 32:29; 34:2, 22).

Jeremiah 23:9–24 and 30:23

The figurative punishment of darkness on the godless prophet and priest
indicates literal disaster (23:12). Further theophanic judgment comes in

---

12. Peter C. Craigie, Page H. Kelley, and Joel F. Drinkard, *Jeremiah 1–25*, WBC
(Dallas: Word, 1991), 82; Jack R. Lundbom, *Jeremiah 1–20*, AB (New York: Doubleday,
1999), 357, on the other hand, correctly notes, "There is, to be sure, in all 'end time' visions
a return of sorts to 'beginning times' . . . but all these visions are rooted in historical events
expected to take place soon, not in some remote future. To this extent, Jeremiah's vision
cannot be called 'apocalyptic.'"

the form of the storm of the Lord which would burst out in wrath, a whirlwind sweeping down on the wicked (23:19). The historical fulfillment of this disaster is undefined, but in the broader context of the surrounding chapters it would surely have been associated with the destruction of the city by the Babylonians. Jeremiah 30:23 repeats the theophanic warning of Jeremiah 23:19 in a context preceded and followed by a description of the return from captivity and blessing.

Jeremiah 43:12–13

God's threat of theophanic fire on the temples of the gods of Egypt is seamlessly merged with the physical fire that Nebuchadnezzar would use to burn the temples of Egypt.

Jeremiah 50–51

Jeremiah 50–51 is an extended prophecy of judgment on Babylon and Babylonia.[13] God will kindle a fire in her towns (50:32), and give rest to the earth but unrest to the inhabitants of Babylon (50:34). Both the theophanic fire and earthquake are figurative of the military action that will be taken against Babylon. Amid this prophecy of judgment there's a theophanic description of Yahweh (51:15–16) as the creator God (51:15) who causes vapors to ascend, makes lightning, and brings rain and wind (51:16). The figurative theophanic description of the land shaking and writhing (51:29) is directly tied to the kings of the Medes (51:28). The sea will flood Babylon and cover her with a multitude of waves (51:42). This flooding is presented literally but meant figuratively. The flood is the human armies that will overwhelm Babylon.

Ezekiel 30:1–19

The Day of the Lord is prophesied against Egypt (v. 3). It will be a day of clouds and doom (v. 3). Yahweh will set fire to Egypt (v. 16). The day will be darkened and she will be covered by a cloud (v. 18). This figurative theophanic judgment language (clouds, darkness, and fire) is explicitly fulfilled by the hand of Nebuchadnezzar king of Babylon

---

13. Gerald L. Keown, Pamela J. Scalise, and Thomas G. Smothers, *Jeremiah 26–52*, WBC 27 (Waco, TX: Word, 1995), 357–73.

(v. 10).[14] The cloud covering Egypt in Ezekiel 30:18 is paired with captivity.

Ezekiel 32:1–16

Ezekiel 32:1–16 is a lament for Pharaoh King of Egypt heavy with theophanic judgment imagery: "When I blot you out, I will cover the heavens and make their stars dark; I will cover the sun with a cloud, and the moon shall not give its light. All the bright lights of heaven will I make dark over you and put darkness on your land, declares the Lord God" (vv. 7–8). All this theophanic judgment language of cosmic darkening is figurative of the destruction that will come by the sword of the king of Babylon (vv. 11–12).

Ezekiel 34:12

Restoration is promised by Yahweh to his sheep who were scattered on a day of clouds and thick darkness. "A day of clouds and darkness" is being used figuratively to describe the fall of Jerusalem and resultant captivity (v. 13).

Ezekiel 38:9, 16

The armies of Gog are described as a cloud covering the land (vv. 9, 16). These are simple examples of the traditional theophanic element of clouds being used as a simile for human armies.

Ezekiel 38:19–22

The prophecy of the destruction of the armies of Gog is full of the vocabulary of theophanic judgment and is qualitatively different from every passage that has been studied so far. The passage is intentionally future oriented. Gog is not a present threat, but rather representative of future threats against God's restored people.[15] Moreover, the theophanic language is not further described as fulfilled by human armies. It may be that as at Sinai, God himself will be the fulfillment of the literal theophanic imagery. There'll be a great earthquake (v. 19), all will tremble, the

---

14. Moshe Greenberg, *Ezekiel 21–37*, AB 22A (New York: Doubleday, 1997), 628 notes that, "The double causality of execution, God working both directly and through human agents, is stressed."

15. See Leslie C. Allen, *Ezekiel 20–48*, WBC 29 (Dallas: Word, 1990), 204–205, for a discussion of the identity of Gog, Meshech, and Tubal.

mountains will be overturned, and cliffs and walls will crumble (v. 20). Rain, sulfur, and hailstones will flood Gog and his armies (v. 22). This passage may refer to the final battle and as such is reflected in Daniel 11:40–45, Revelation 20:7–10, and "became a firm part of Jewish eschatology in rabbinic tradition."[16]

Hosea 8:14

Yahweh will send fire upon the fortified cities of Judah which will devour his palaces. In conjunction with this judgment of Judah, verse 13 mentions a "return to Egypt" for Israel, figuratively pointing to a return to slavery fulfilled by the Assyrian captivity.[17] While not explicitly developed in Hosea 8 Yahweh's theophanic fire of judgment would have figuratively pointed to the physical Assyrian invasion of Judah by Sennacherib in 701.[18]

Hosea 13:15–16

An east wind, the wind of Yahweh, will come from the wilderness and dry up the springs and fountains of Samaria (vv. 15–16). This destructive wind is further described as a plundering of the treasury and death by sword (vv. 15–16). The infants will be dashed to pieces and pregnant women will be ripped open (v. 16). The theophanic destructive wind from Yahweh is figurative of the carnage of physical military destruction. Assyria is Yahweh's destructive east wind.[19]

Joel 1:1–2:27

Space precludes a full discussion of many important aspects of the book of Joel including its date and the identification of the locust armies (human or locust).[20] These and other questions can be bypassed due to the

---

16. Ibid., 210.

17. Theodore Ferdinand Karl Laetsch, *Minor Prophets*, CCCS (St. Louis: Concordia, 1987), 72.

18. Chisholm, *Handbook on the Prophets*, 358.

19. Laetsch, *Minor Prophets*, 107.

20. See Chisholm, *Handbook on the Prophets*, 368–77; Leslie C. Allen, *The Books of Joel, Obadiah, Jonah, and Micah*, NICOT (Grand Rapids: Eerdmans, 1976), 19–126; Graham S. Ogden and Richard Deutsch, *A Promise of Hope, a Call to Obedience: A Commentary on the Books of Joel and Malachi*, ITC (Grand Rapids: Eerdmans, 1987), 3–60; David Allan Hubbard, *Joel and Amos*, TOTC (Leicester: InterVarsity, 1989), 21–86; John D. W. Watts,

focused nature of this study on the fulfillment of theophanic judgment vocabulary. Chapter 1 points to a historical drought and locust invasion as the destructive judgment of the day of the Lord. Joel 2:1–11 describes the horror of a presumed future day of the Lord which would be fulfilled by either locusts or invading human armies. The people apparently respond to the warning with repentance and Yahweh relents and sends a blessing instead (2:18–27).

The Day of the Lord threatened in 2:1–11 will cause all the inhabitants of the land to tremble (v. 1). It'll be a day of darkness, gloom, clouds, and thick clouds (v. 2). Before the army (locust or human) of the day of the Lord the earth shakes, the heavens quake, the sun and moon grow dark, and stars withdraw their brightness (v. 10). The earthquakes and cosmic darkening mentioned in 2:1–2 is explicitly connected with the physical army of locusts or humans who are the cause of the earthquake and cosmic darkness of 2:10. It's true that Yahweh utters his voice before his army, but in 2:10 the theophanic vocabulary of judgment is attributed to the physical army itself.[21]

Joel 2:28–32

The coming of the Spirit on all flesh (v. 28) before the coming eschatological Day of the Lord (v. 31) will be accompanied by wonders in the heavens and earth: blood, fire, and columns of smoke (v. 30).[22] The sun will be turned to darkness, and the moon to blood (v. 31). Canonically, this was fulfilled by the outpouring of the Holy Spirit on the day of Pentecost (Acts 2:14–21). Peter's interpretation of Joel 2:28–32 indicates that he saw no problem with the fact that the cosmic events of Joel 2:30–31 were not literally fulfilled on that day because they were figuratively fulfilled in the powerful outpouring of the Holy Spirit.[23] It seems that Peter understood and interpreted Joel's language of cosmic upheaval to be primarily figurative.

The Books of Joel, Obadiah, Jonah, Nahum, Habakkuk, and Zephaniah, CBC (Cambridge: Cambridge University Press, 1975), 12–50.

21 Watts, *Books of Joel, Obadiah, Jonah, Nahum, Habakkuk, and Zephaniah*, 26; Ogden and Deutsch, *A Promise of Hope, a Call to Obedience*, 29.

22. Hubbard, *Joel and Amos*, 71, rightly draws a connection between this description and the Exodus and Sinai theophanies.

23. Allen, *Books of Joel, Obadiah, Jonah, and Micah*, 103, rightly seeks to argue that to some extent the prophecy was fulfilled literally in the darkening of the sky during the crucifixion with the result that the moon may have looked red in the afternoon. It's very

Joel 3:15–16

The final chapter of Joel contains prophecies of judgment against Tyre and Sidon (v. 4), and Egypt and Edom (v. 19). As against his own people, the day of the Lord will come against these nations with theophanic elements. When Yahweh judges these nations the sun and moon will grow dark, the stars will withdraw their brightness (v. 15), and the heavens and earth will shake (v. 16). The historic judgment of these nations came by way of foreign invading armies without literal theophanic earthquakes and cosmic darkening.

Amos 1:1–2:5

Amos 1:3–2:5 consists of a series of judgment speeches against various nations united by their focus on divine fire as punishment.[24] Yahweh will send a devouring fire on Damascus (1:4), Gaza (1:7), Tyre (1:10), Edom (1:12), Ammon (1:14), Moab (2:2), and Judah (2:5).[25] Ammon is singled out by a further emphasis on a storm in the day of whirlwind (Amos 2:14). Elements of fulfillment of the divine theophanic fire include the people of Syria going captive to Kir (Amos 1:5), shouting in the day of battle (1:14), captivity (1:15), and tumult, shouting and the sound of a trumpet (2:2). Although the judgments against Gaza, Tyre, Edom, and Judah don't include explicit references to human warfare it can safely be inferred from the other judgment speeches that the fulfillment of divine fire (along with the storm and whirlwind) will come in the physical fire and destruction of conquering armies.[26]

Amos 5:18–20

Amos corrects the common misconception among the Israelites that the day of the Lord would be a day of salvation. Instead, because of their sin, it would be a day of darkness and gloom. The day of the Lord arrived with finality for the Northern kingdom in the form of Assyrian armies in 722 BC.

---

likely that the early church did view that as the fulfillment of the prophecy, but such a fulfillment still requires a figurative interpretation of blood, fire, and clouds of smoke.

24. The judgment speech against Israel (2:5–16) does not highlight divine fire.

25. Hubbard, *Joel and Amos*, 127–40.

26. See Chisholm, *Handbook on the Prophets*, 381–84, for an account of the historical fulfillment of each of these prophecies.

Amos 8:8–9 and 9:1–6

Amos 1:1 explicitly locates Amos's ministry two years before a specific earthquake (cf. Zech 14:5) during the reigns of Uzziah king of Judah and Jeroboam king of Israel. Amos 8:8 warns that because of their deeds the land will tremble. Amos 9:1–6 proceeds to describe a coming earthquake with a prophecy of the thresholds shaking (v. 1) and a description of Yahweh who touches the earth and causes it to melt and swell (v. 5). It's very likely that the original recipients viewed the earthquake mentioned in Amos 1:1 as fulfillment of the prophesied earthquake of 8:8 and 9:1–6. Counting against this connection however, is the fact that the quaking described in 9:1–6 is directly connected with slaying the last of them with the sword (v. 1), and a captivity in which the sword will continue to slay (v. 4). The sword and captivity didn't strike the Northern kingdom during the time of the historic earthquake mentioned in 1:1 (753 BC at the latest).[27] The historical earthquake was a physical forerunner to the destruction caused by the "earthquake" of Assyrian armies.

Amos 8:9 adds a description of cosmic darkness to the judgment that will come "in that day." The sun will go down at noon and the earth will be darkened in broad daylight. There were recorded solar eclipses in 784 and 763 BC that Amos and his hearers would have remembered, but neither of those events could have been the fulfillment of the darkness prophesied by Amos associated with the coming day of judgment.[28] The fulfillment of Amos's prophesied theophanic darkness of judgment would have been the fall of Samaria in 722 BC.

Micah 1:4

Micah 1:3–7 portrays a theophanic visit by God in judgment on Samaria and Jerusalem for their sins. Yahweh will come down causing the mountains to melt and the valleys to split before his fire. The historical fulfillment of this figurative theophany is the reduction of Samaria to a heap of ruins (Micah 1:6) and captivity and exile (1:16).[29] Yahweh's visitation in

---

27. Hubbard, *Joel and Amos*, 89–90, notes a broad consensus based on both internal and external evidence that Amos's ministry took place between 760 and 755 BC. Two years after this later date give 753 BC as the latest date for the earthquake, thirty-one years before the destruction of Samaria by the Assyrian armies in 722 BC.

28. Ibid., 222.

29. Ralph L. Smith, *Micah-Malachi*, WBC 32 (Waco, TX: Word, 1984), 18, discusses

judgment on his people by the Assyrians and Babylonians was not physically accompanied by the theophanic melting of mountains by fire, but
rather through captivity and the devastation of war.[30]

Nahum 1:1–8

The theophanic description of Yahweh in Nahum 1:3b–5 functions to
assert "that Yahweh is sovereign over all creation and capable of exercising authority in it."[31] Yahweh has his way in the whirlwind and storm
and the clouds are the dust of his feet (v. 3b). He dries up the land, sea,
and rivers (v. 4). The mountains quake, hills melt, and the earth and
all who dwell in it heave before him (v. 5). His wrath is poured out like
fire and rocks are broken to pieces before him (v. 6). An overflowing
flood will make an end of "its place" (i.e. Nineveh; cf. 1:1; 2:8; 3:7) and
darkness will pursue his enemies (v. 8). After such a description who
would doubt that Yahweh could execute the full punishment of Nineveh
described in the book of Nahum? The destruction of Nineveh came in
612 BC at the hands of Babylonian armies without the presence of literal
theophanic elements.

Zephaniah 1:15

The Day of the Lord against Jerusalem in Zephaniah 1:15 is described as
a day of wrath, trouble, distress, devastation, desolation, darkness, gloom,
clouds, and thick clouds.[32] The whole land will be consumed by the fire of
Yahweh's jealousy (1:18; cf. 3:8). This clear reminiscence of Sinai is fulfilled

---

the historical fulfillment of this prophecy. "In 722/21 B.C. Samaria was captured by the
Assyrians. At that time the city experienced little physical damage. It certainly was not
destroyed. Sargon II, King of Assyria, claims to have restored the city and made it more
habitable than before. The restored city served as the capital of the province of Samaria
until its capture by Alexander the Great. Then it became a Greek city with pagan shrines.
It was destroyed by John Hyrcanus ca 107 B.C. but was soon rebuilt. It has been occupied
constantly since that date."

30. Allen, *Books of Joel, Obadiah, Jonah, and Micah*, 268, also notes that, "The allusion
to fire in v. 7 suggests military invasion, as does the tenor of the latter part of the verse."

31. Smith, *Micah-Malachi*, 74.

32. O. Palmer Robertson, *The Books of Nahum, Habakkuk, and Zephaniah*, NICOT
(Grand Rapids: Eerdmans, 1990), 283, comments on the connection between this
description and the Sinai theophany.

in Zephaniah by trumpets and battle cry against fortified cities and high towers (1:16; i.e., literal destruction by foreign armies).[33]

Haggai 2:6–7, 21

Yahweh promises that in a little while he will shake the heaven, earth, sea, dry land, and all nations (vv. 6–7; cf. 2:21). While this shaking is not linked explicitly to historic warfare and may have eschatological overtones, Haggai 2:22 explains it to be the overthrowing of the thrones of kingdoms, chariots, horses and riders each by the sword of his brother, indicating human battle.[34]

Zechariah 7:14

Zechariah 7:14 recollects Yahweh's great wrath in scattering his people with a whirlwind among all the nations.[35] Yahweh's whirlwind was the physical army of the Babylonians carrying the people into exile and captivity.

Zechariah 9:14

God will march in the storms of the south in battle in support of Judah and Ephraim against the Greeks. Even though the historical setting for the fulfillment of this prophecy is debatable the theophanic storm is figurative for Yahweh's aid in physical battle.[36]

Summary

The cumulative effect of the verses surveyed in this Appendix is that the theophanic vocabulary of judgment and disaster in the Hebrew prophets is primarily figurative of the destruction caused by physical armies and human warfare. This conclusion is amply supported by the texts. Earthquakes, storms, darkness, and fire are prophesied in historic contexts where the fulfillment is clearly at the hands of human

---

33. Adele Berlin, *Zephaniah*, AB 25a (New York: Doubleday, 1994), 90. Cf. Exodus 20:21; Deuteronomy 4:11; 2 Samuel 22:10; 1 Kings 8:12; Psalm 18:9 [10]; Psalm 97:2.

34. Carl Friedrich Keil and Franz Delitzsch, *The Twelve Minor Prophets*, vol. 2, BCOT (Edinburgh: T & T Clark, 1868), 192, rightly draw attention to the fact that the shaking of nations in 2:7 and 2:22 points to wars, revolutions, and political convulsions.

35. See Smith, *Micah-Malachi*, 225, for some comments on the tense of the verb. It is grammatically future, but the surrounding verbs point to the past.

36. Keil and Delitzsch, *Twelve Minor Prophets*, 341, point to the Jewish understanding of the fulfillment of this passage in the wars between the Maccabees and the Seleucids.

armies apart from literal theophanic help. It's true the earthquakes, storms, and cosmic phenomena (e.g., solar eclipses) have taken place throughout history and were attributed to the activity of deity in the ancient world, but the actual fulfillment of the prophecies made by the Hebrew prophets (the fall of Samaria, Jerusalem, Nineveh, Babylon, Egypt, Edom, etc.) took place by the clear secondary means of physical, human agents.

Lundbom, commenting on Jeremiah 4:23–28, provides a helpful description of the prophetic, figurative, hyperbolic language surveyed in this Appendix:

> There is, to be sure, in all "end time" visions a return of sorts to "beginning times" . . . but all these visions are rooted in historical events expected to take place soon, not in some remote future. To this extent, Jeremiah's vision cannot be called "apocalyptic." . . . It seems better to speak here of "prophetic hyperbole." Jeremiah, like the other prophets, uses his great poetic imagination to describe a destruction of staggering proportions, the horrors of which can perhaps be conveyed in no other way. Images describing such a reality naturally overstate, but less imaginative images will understate.[37]

The designation "imaginative prophetic hyperbole" seems on target. The shared prophetic vocabulary of judgment communicated concepts of theophanic judgment and disaster that were consistently rooted and fulfilled historically by human armies. This conclusion doesn't affect the literal historicity of actual recorded theophanies in the Hebrew Scriptures, nor does it negate the literal theophanic elements of eschatology proper when Christ will return with finality to judge and save.[38] The imaginative, figurative, hyperbolic elements of prophetic theophanies are firmly grounded in literal, historic theophanies and typologically foreshadow a coming final, literal, eschatological theophany.

---

37. Lundbom, *Jeremiah 1–20*, 357.

38. See Niehaus, *God at Sinai*, 316–31 and 344–53, for a discussion of eschatologically oriented passages such as Daniel 7:9–10; 10:1–12:13 and the book of Revelation.

Conclusion

A close study of the Old Testament prophets indicates that the language of cosmic upheaval was used to describe God's judgment of cities and nations through the normal means of human armies and warfare. The language of cosmic upheaval in the Old Testament is linked to the language of theophany (the appearance of God) and stresses the theological truth that God himself was active in the judgment of these cities. If Jesus were using the language of cosmic upheaval in the Olivet Discourse in continuity with the Hebrew prophets, it could very naturally apply to the destruction of Jerusalem. It is also evident, however, that some first-century Jews and Christians understood that physical and literal cosmic upheaval would indeed characterize the final day of judgment, and it is not at all evident that such language should be understood figuratively when applied to Jesus' second coming.[39] The Old Testament background discussed in this Appendix is thus informative but not conclusive in determining Jesus' intention when using the language of cosmic upheaval in the Olivet Discourse.

---

39. 2 Peter 3:10; Hebrews 12:26–27; Revelation 6:12–14; 20:11; 4 Ezra 7:30, 38–42.

Appendix 2

The Future at a Glance

Matthew				
Persecution	Growing Conflict Leading to the Imminent Judgment of This Generation in the Year 70	The Coming of the Son of Man and the Unspecified Period Preceding the Parousia	Future Resurrection	Final Judgment, Eternal Reward and Punishment
5:10–12 10:16–23, 24–25 13:21 16:24–26	3:7–10, 12 8:11–12 9:3, 11, 34 10:16–24 11:16–19, 20–24 12:1–8, 9–14, 24–32, 34, 38–42, 43–45 13:10–15, 57–58 15:1–9, 12–14 16:1–4, 5–12 17:17 21:12–16, 23–27, 28–32, 33–46 22:1–10, 15–22, 34–35 23:1–39 24:1–28, 32–35 26:3–5 Predictions of Death and Resurrection: 16:21; 17:9, 12, 22–23; 20:17–19; 26:2, 12	10:23 16:27–28 24:29–31, 36–51 25:1–13, 14–30, 31 26:64	8:11–12 22:23–33 26:29	5:22, 29–30 6:20 7:21–23 8:11–12 10:28–33 12:36, 41–42 13:36–43, 47–50 18:7–9 19:16–21

Mark				
Persecution	Growing Conflict Leading to the Imminent Judgment of This Generation in the Year 70	The Coming of the Son of Man and the Unspecified Period Preceding the Parousia	Future Resurrection	Final Judgment, Eternal Reward and Punishment
4:17 8:34–38 10:28–31	2:16–17, 23–28 3:1–6, 22–30 7:6–13 8:11–12, 38 9:19 11:12–22 12:1–12, 38–40 Predictions of Death and Resurrection: 8:31; 9:9, 12, 31; 10:34, 45; 14:21, 41	11:12–22 12:1–12, 38–40	12:18–27	8:38–9:2 14:62 12:18–27

Luke				
Persecution	Growing Conflict Leading to the Imminent Judgment of This Generation in the Year 70	The Coming of the Son of Man and the Unspecified Period Preceding the Parousia	Future Resurrection	Final Judgment, Eternal Reward and Punishment
6:22–23 8:13 9:23–25 12:4–7, 11–12	3:8–9, 17 5:21, 30 6:2, 7 7:30–35 9:40–41 10:13–15 11:15–16, 29–32, 37–54 12:1 13:14, 34–35 14:15–24 15:1–2 16:14–15 19:41–44 20:9–18, 45–47 23:28–31 Predictions of Death and Resurrection: 9:22, 44; 12:50; 13:32–33; 17:25; 18:32–33; 22:22; 24:6–7, 25–26, 46	1:32–33 9:26–29 12:35–48 17:20–37 18:8 19:11–27	12:4–7 14:13–14 20:27–40	10:13–15 11:29–32 12:4–7, 8–9 13:27–30 16:22–26 18:30 22:16, 18, 28–30

John					
Future Persecution	Escalating Conflict	Son of Man	Future Resurrection & Final Judgment	Preparing a Place in the Father's House	Resurrection & New Creation
15:18–16:4	5:17–18	1:51	3:18	14:1–3	18:1, 26
	6:60–71	3:13–14	5:19-29		19:5, 41
	10:30–31	5:27	11:1–44		20:1, 15, 19,
	19:7	6:27, 53, 62	12:31		22, 26
		8:28			
		9:35			
		12:23, 34			
		13:31			

Subject Index

Scripture Index

Old Testament

New Testament

Author Index